A HEALING
FELLOWSHIP

A HEALING FELLOWSHIP

A guide to practical counselling in the local church

Mary Pytches

HODDER AND STOUGHTON
LONDON SYDNEY AUCKLAND TORONTO

Quotations from the Bible are from the New International Version unless otherwise stated.

British Library Cataloguing in Publication Data

Pytches, Mary
   A healing fellowship: a guide to
practical counselling in the local church.
1. Christian church. Pastoral work.
Counselling
I. Title
253.5

   ISBN 0 340 48701 1

Printed in Great Britain for Hodder and Stoughton Limited, Mill Road, Dunton Green, Sevenoaks, Kent by Cox & Wyman Ltd, Reading, Berks. Typeset by Hewer Text Composition Services, Edinburgh.

Hodder and Stoughton Editorial Office: 47 Bedford Square, London WC1B 3DP.

CONTENTS

INTRODUCTION

The demand for counselling in the local church is on the increase. We regularly receive heart-rending requests for help. How can we begin to meet this wider need without grinding to a standstill? The answer can only be by encouraging and teaching others "to go and do likewise".

In my first book, *Set My People Free*, I shared what we are learning at St. Andrew's Chorleywood about the ministry of inner healing. *A Healing Fellowship* enlarges on some aspects of the first in response to questions arising from it. I also share from new experience in ministering and constant thinking on the whole subject of counselling.

John Wimber visited St. Andrew's in 1981 and began to teach us how to minister to the sick in the power of the Holy Spirit. One of his parting remarks to my husband was "whatever you have received, give it away to others".

This we have sought to do. Everything that God has given to us in the way of blessing, insights and ministry we have tried to share with others. This book is about giving away the ministry of counselling in the hope that many more churches will begin providing "a safe place" where hurting people can find some measure of healing.

Inner healing takes place in a person's life when the Holy Spirit brings to the surface an unresolved issue, which has been previously repressed or suppressed, in order to bring a resolution. These unresolved issues include such things as unconfessed sin, broken relationships, unhealed hurts, inner vows, wrong choices and attitudes. The healing or resolution may happen whenever or wherever the Holy Spirit is invited to come and minister in power. This could be unplanned and unexpected, as may happen in a large gathering or small group meeting. It could also happen in the more intentional and arranged environment of the counselling room. In the former it is an incidental sovereign ministry performed by anyone who has some experience of praying for the sick. The latter, however, is a ministry which involves counselling as well as inner healing. It is executed by those with a special aptitude who have been set aside by the leadership of the church for this ministry. It is a longer, planned ministry and seeks to address the various unresolved issues in a person's life which have caused personality problems and have had an adverse effect on everyday living.

One of the aims in writing *Set My People Free* was to encourage the ministry of inner healing to be done in its rightful place – the fellowship of the local church. In *A Healing Fellowship* one aim has been to highlight the need for safety in counselling. The counselling relationship has within it the potential for encouraging and fostering maturity in people but there are some major difficulties in this relationship which need to be recognised and, if possible, avoided.

Secondly, the role of catharsis in emotional healing is also explored and discussed. In our ministry we have sought always to follow the Holy Spirit's leading – to track God and allow Him room and time to work in people's lives. This practice has led us increasingly to see the benefit of allowing for, and even encouraging a counsellee fully to express his feelings about painful incidents in his past. Catharsis is not in itself healing, but it would appear to be an important element in the healing process. It opens up the painful closed off areas of a person's life enabling the Holy Spirit to penetrate with healing. With appropriate ministry a proper closure or resolution to the past experience can be achieved. The past cannot be changed but inner healing and counselling can change the way we view it and our reaction to it.

"Counselling is one way of opening up the past in a safe environment so that it can be faced, renegotiated and in some respects even relived but with a new ending" (*The Presenting Past*, Michael Jacobs).

Finally some of the different opinions surrounding the ministry of inner healing are examined.

Once again I must express my gratitude to my husband David who all the way along has been my encourager and helpful critic. Also, to my colleagues and fellow counsellors, I owe a debt of gratitude. I have learned so much from our shared experience. As before I must thank those who have trusted us with their inner conflicts and pain. It has been a privilege to work with them and learn from them. It is to these brave people that I dedicate this book.

I offer it with the prayer that it may be of some help and encouragement to churches, who like us, are already attempting, in some poor way, to "bind up the broken-hearted". I pray too that more churches will feel encouraged to initiate such a ministry. However, when all is said and done, it is simply a book written by a lay person for lay people. It is a book about "a safe place" where people are free to feel their feelings, to cry, to laugh, to discover their real selves and finally to be ministered to by the Holy Spirit, who brings forgiveness and healing to us through Jesus Christ and builds us up in our relationship with God the Father, and our fellowship with each other.

1

A HEALING COMMUNITY

It was a Saturday night celebration and people were praying in groups around the church. Some were kneeling, others sitting on the floor, some standing. There was laughter, tears and quiet sharing. The power of God was present to heal the sick.

As I watched all this take place I remembered what Jesus had said to His disciples as He sent them out two by two. "When you enter a town and are welcomed, eat what is set before you. Heal the sick who are there and tell them, 'The kingdom of God is near you'" (Luke 10:8, 9). Their healing ministry was a demonstration of the presence of the Kingdom.

Jesus showed what the Kingdom was like through His miracles. He taught what it was like through His parables. As I thought of the Kingdom coming near as we heal the sick the parable Jesus told about the grain of mustard seed came to mind (Mark 4:30–34). The tiniest of all seeds grew and became the largest of the garden plants "with such big branches that the birds of the air can perch in its shade." In this parable Jesus was giving us yet another slant on the Kingdom of God.

Besides speaking of its growth potential, whereby it starts very small but ends up, in comparison to other plants, very large, He is also showing us its potential as a refuge. The birds of the air could perch and find shade in its branches, even though it was only a garden plant. Some commentators see the birds of the air as something sinister. Taken at its face value, however, without trying to read too

11

much into it, the picture is one of growth and refuge in the Kingdom of God. It was the latter aspect of the Kingdom as a refuge that came to me as I watched those people ministering to one another.

I reflected on the small beginnings of this healing ministry a few years previously. It was as if the seed had been sown, had taken root and grown; slowly at times, faster at others. Now in comparison the growth was obvious, even amazing. As I witnessed the power of God moving upon the people at that service I knew the Kingdom was there. Not yet in all its fullness of course, but certainly the "Kingdom to come" had broken through into this present age and we were experiencing a foretaste of its glory – a glory where, when it fully comes, "there will be no more death or mourning or crying or pain" (Rev. 21:4). However, right there and then, people were experiencing the love and mercy of Christ's Kingdom in their lives. For a time their tears were dried, their pain was eased. Surely these were tokens of the day when we shall all be fully freed and healed. I saw, too, the potential for refuge that the Kingdom has. The Swiss sociologist Christian Lalive d'Epinay encapsulates this reality with his study of Chilean Pentecostalism in the 1960s through the title for his book _The Haven of the Masses_. The church here too was becoming a haven for the wounded and hurting, the battered, the weary and the sick. They had come and found rest, refreshment and healing. In so doing I felt it was reflecting a little of the Kingdom in this place.

A Pentecost visitation

This healing ministry, as it is today, had its beginnings the weekend of Pentecost 1981, when an American team visited the church. I remember during that evening standing with my hands towards a person with a bad back praying for her healing. As I did so I became uncomfortably aware that my hands were burning so much that they actually hurt me. Then to my amazement I heard the speaker ask for those with burning hands to come forward because God was anointing them for a ministry to the sick. Standing in line with some twenty others I had a feeling of awe as oil was poured on to my burning hands and the gift of healing confirmed. From that moment I felt totally committed to the exercise of this ministry whatever it would lead to.

That initial outpouring led on to establishing regular "teach-ins" on ministering in the power of the Holy Spirit; to praying for the sick at every major public service and to encouraging ministry to one another at other more informal gatherings, such as home groups. It has also become our church's policy to give this ministry away to others with teams going out far and wide, sharing what God has given them. A further off-shoot of that initial anointing has been a ministry of inner healing and prayer counselling undertaken by laypeople with a special aptitude for it.

Real community

Many other results of that powerful pentecost visitation could be listed. Changes in individual lives have been remarkable but the most notable have been observed in our corporate life together. There has been a gradual lowering of the masks and a pulling down of the defences behind which most of us live. This has led to a growing atmosphere of openness, acceptance and vulnerability. Out of this openness has come a growing sense of real community in the body of Christ.

In his latest book, *The Different Drum*, the North American Dr Scott Peck explores the healing to be found where true community exists. He quotes the first governor of the Massachusetts Bay Colony, John Winthrop, who in 1630 addressed his fellow colonist just prior to setting foot on land. "We must delight in each other, make others' conditions our own, rejoice together, mourn together, labour and suffer together, always having before our eyes

our community as members of the same body." That
echoes the spirit of true community.

"A community is a union of persons who 'have in
common,' who share in mutuality their most precious
possessions – themselves. They know and are open to one
another. They share in love their persons and their lives"
(*Fully Human, Fully Alive*, John Powell).

In today's hurting world there is an increasing need for
the security of a true community or a church that will
manifest the qualities of the Kingdom of God; in particular
that of being a refuge. It is a sad reflection on the church
that it so seldom meets this need. One of the major reasons
for that is pretence. We have grown up in a society where
masks are deliberately cultivated. "Don't let people know
how you feel." "Keep yourself to yourself." "Keep up a
good front." A frantically scribbled note passed along to
my husband at a recent conference in Europe says it all
quaintly but succinctly. "I felt like I'm inside a big stone . . .
I wanted to leave your meeting. I felt an outsider and I did
not believe it's the Lord. I'm afraid to let the Holy Spirit
come because I'm afraid of losing my control – I never let
other people see my pain."

These practices have been incorporated into our church
lives. We don't recognise them as unchristian because they
have become so much a part of our western culture.
Anything else seems abnormal, even shameful! Instead of
truth, vulnerability and openness, masks and unreality are
the order of the day. Pretence is the name of the game.

Peter Lomas suggests that a person often has no recourse
but to turn to psychotherapy because of the lack of
"another society, one in which people would feel more able
to be intimate, more ready to turn to others than seeking
out an expert of some kind and more able to expose their
weaknesses without fear of ridicule or condemnation."
Sadly, he comments, "we do not live in such a society" (*A
Case for Personal Psychotherapy*).

There is an urgent need for the Christian Church to be a
demonstration of this alternative society. In the Bible we

read, "God is light, there is no darkness in Him at all – no, not in any way. So if we say we are partakers together and enjoy fellowship with Him when we live and move and are walking about in darkness, we are (both) speaking falsely and do not live and practice the Truth (of the Gospel). But if we (really) are living and walking in the Light as He (Himself) is in the Light, we have (true, unbroken) fellowship with one another, and the blood of Jesus Christ His Son cleanses (removes) us from all sin and guilt – keeps us cleansed from sin and all its forms and manifestations" (1 John 1:5–7, Amplified Version). Walking in honesty and openness with one another will produce Kingdom relationships and fellowship. Real community will replace the pretence that so often exists.

Pseudocommunity

"In pseudocommunity a group attempts to purchase community cheaply by pretence. It is not an evil, conscious pretence of deliberate black lies. Rather, it is an unconscious, gentle process whereby people who want to be loving attempt to be so by telling little white lies, by withholding some of the truth about themselves and their feelings in order to avoid conflict. But it is still a pretence. It is an inviting but illegitimate shortcut to nowhere" (*The Different Drum*, Dr Scott Peck).

Basically pseudocommunity is a group of people living a lie together in silent consensus. It is a community diametrically opposed to true Christian community whose hallmarks should be those of truth and love. Pseudocommunity can never really heal. There will be no safe place within such a church for the hurting and disturbed people who come there hopefully seeking relief.

The breakthrough from pseudo to real

If the Church is to become the refuge and haven for which we all hunger and yearn, its members will have to break through the pain barrier and become authentic human beings.

Sometimes God instigates the breakthrough sovereignly and sends His Holy Spirit with power so that carefully erected defences crumble. The pentecost I described was such an occasion. I remember whole families weeping together as the Holy Spirit touched them. Children were ministering to their parents and parents to their children. Since then one of the most moving occurrences has been to see whole families kneeling at the communion rails after a service asking for God's help or married couples humbly asking God to help them draw closer to one another.

Sometimes God uses one person to make the breakthrough into reality. Usually for this to happen it has to be a significant person in the church. Someone who cannot easily be ignored.

One evening service I was sitting next to someone who has a significant ministry in the church here. She is a skilled counsellor who has always appeared an emotionally stable person. During a time of prayer she began to cry, fairly quietly at first. I put my hand out to comfort but the crying increased. I prayed silently wondering whatever was wrong. As I did so I sensed she was expressing deep intercessory prayer for a person I knew she was particularly concerned about. On perceiving this I began to bless what God was doing in her. Immediately the crying became stronger and much noisier – so much so that many people were looking around and, recognising who it was, seemed distinctly disturbed. Her sobbing continued as we queued to take the communion. The emotion increased even more as she took the cup, after which it subsided. At the end of the service people began to share their feelings. "I was so scared," said one. "I could hardly bear it," said another. On hearing the reason for the tears one man said that he wished he could be sufficiently uninhibited to respond to God so freely!

These responses were all indicative of people growing towards true community. They were disturbed and even afraid, but instead of moving away from the cause of their discomfort they bravely admitted to the feelings and moved in close to the person concerned. They felt they had received permission to dare to be real through witnessing someone they respected being real.

Another way a breakthrough may be achieved is by a home group, a prayer group or Bible study group becoming open and real with one another. Like the leaven in the dough which slowly and imperceptibly affects the whole lump, so can a small group affect the larger body.

Once the barriers are down and the pretence gone, the Church will become a healing community and it will draw hurting people to it. Some of these will be healed by just being part of the family. Others will need some special care.

In a maternity hospital all the babies need loving care and attention but some need a special care unit for a time, where they can receive individual attention. So in the Church family a special care unit is sometimes needed to deal with the sort of problems that cannot be solved within the ordinary family.

It is this special place that we shall now look at in more detail before we move on to consider the practical ways we can ensure the safety of those who receive counsel there.

2

A SAFE PLACE

As a child growing up in Devon I loved to climb trees. Living in the country I knew every tree in the vicinity that was climbable. I knew the branches intimately and had special places in some of the trees where I could be safely hidden from view. Those were places of refuge for me and I spent many silent hours reflecting, usually ensconced there with a book. It was as if the trees held out their arms to me and embraced me, taking me into their shade and providing me with a safe hiding place. Our upper room, where the ministry of inner healing and prayer counselling so often occurs, is such a place. It has embraced and taken in many desperate and hurting people who have found refuge there.

Had we recorded every encounter that had taken place in that upper room how many different stories of hurt, deprivation and sin could be told? One comment, however, remains imprinted on my memory because it has been repeated so frequently. "I feel safe here." As soon as I hear that I begin to sense that this person will eventually find some real healing and freedom from whatever troubles him.

There is a good explanation for this intuitive feeling of hope. Human beings have a natural yearning and thrust toward health. "Most of the time, however, this thrust, this energy, is enchained by fear, neutralised by defenses and resistances, but put a human being in a truly safe place, where these defenses and resistances are no longer necessary, and the thrust toward health is liberated. When we are safe, there is a natural tendency for us to heal and convert ourselves" (*The Different Drum*, Dr Scott Peck).

A letter we received from a recent visitor to our church confirms this statement:

> At the end of the evening worship Jesus led two of your team to pray with me and I was able to share my burden of disbelief and rebellion and my fear of whole-hearted commitment, whilst longing and asking that this be removed.
>
> Through their ministry I experienced Jesus' love through the Holy Spirit, physically, emotionally and spiritually.
>
> I want to take this opportunity to thank you and your team for providing a 'safe place' for long term anglicans like me to meet the Lord.
>
> It was those words 'this is a safe place, a sanctuary' that were contributory to my release.

Safety is vital for healing and growth.

In her challenging and moving story Virginia Axline gives us a glimpse into "the wonderful playroom" where six-year-old Dibs finds such safety. He begins his therapy very grimly, "a child trapped in a prison of fear and rage". But gradually as the weeks progress he begins to find the way to freedom. Some of his comments about his time in the "wonderful playroom", as he calls her therapy room, indicate how truly it becomes a place of refuge and healing for him.

"At first the playroom seemed so big, very big," he said. "And the toys were not friendly. And I was afraid." And again, "I was frightened . . . because I didn't know what you would do and I didn't know what I would do. But you just said, 'this is all yours Dibs. Have fun. Nobody is going to hurt you in here.'"

Another time he told Miss A, "In here I am safe, you won't let anything hurt me."

As Dibs' sense of security increased he was able to explore his frightening feelings. He relived them painfully and expressed them sometimes violently, sometimes sorrowfully. As he learned to express his feelings he also learned to control them. At the end of therapy he was able to say, "The little boy is gone now, but big Dibs is big and strong and brave. He is not afraid anymore" (*Dibs, In Search of Self*, Virginia Axline).

Safety and freedom

For Dibs to grow up and learn to deal with his terrors he needed the security of the "wonderful playroom". For one hour every week the playroom became his haven, a place where he filled up with happiness and strength. Safety for Dibs gave him the freedom to explore his painful feelings.

Safe boundaries are very important if we are to explore potentially dangerous areas of our lives, as the following little story illustrates.

Once upon a time there was a small island rising steeply out of the ocean. The edge of the island was surrounded with strong fencing, protecting the islanders from accidentally falling over the sheer cliff face into the sea. Within these boundaries the islanders lived normal, happy lives. One day a boat arrived at the island and some sailors came ashore, staying with the islanders for a number of weeks. While there the sailors mocked the natives for the protective fence. "You live like prisoners behind your fence. Take it down and then you will be free," they said. At first the islanders protested but eventually they were persuaded and removed the fence. The sailors left soon after.

A year later they returned and to their amazement found the inhabitants huddled together in the very centre of the island. Their eyes were darting nervously around as they sought to keep their families constantly within view. The boundary fence was gone and so too was their sense of security. With the protection of the fence they had known complete freedom to live and work with ease. Safety goes hand in hand with freedom.

The need for boundaries is applicable to all areas of life. God gave His people the ten commandments out of love for them. He was outlining the boundaries within which they could live happily with each other. Jude reflects this when he writes "stay always within the boundaries where God's love can reach and bless you" (verse 21, Living Bible). Some, like the sailors, see boundaries as a limitation but others like the islanders find them a protection behind which they feel secure.

Safe counselling

In the counselling room, boundaries are vital if a counsellee is to feel safe and make full use of the time. He comes there for the first time with very little idea of what is expected of him. Like Dibs he could say, "I didn't know what you would do, and I didn't know what I would do." The counsellee comes with trepidation. He is unsure of his reception. Will he be accepted – warts and all? Will he be treated with kindness and respect or will he be criticised and put down? He is risking a great deal by asking for help. Therefore it is impossible for him to set the boundaries and to provide the safe place. These must be set and clarified by the counsellor in the first instance. But once set, understood and agreed to, the responsibility for keeping within them belongs to both counsellee and counsellor. As we shall see both parties in fact need the protection of these boundaries.

The counsellor's first task then, is to provide a haven where an emotionally sick person can find healing. He must prepare the place and himself with this in view. Everything should be done to ensure that the counsellee finds real healing not further hurt. Already he has been the victim of his own and others' sin. It is a serious business being involved in another person's search for wholeness. Sometimes we fail to alleviate the mental and emotional suffering and seem unable to minister the healing power of

Christ to a person's life. Nevertheless it would be unforgivable if by any oversight or thoughtlessness on our part a counsellee should leave our time together more damaged than he came.

The goal for safe counselling

At first Dibs' only safety was the playroom. He cried on leaving it and counted the days until he came back – relieved that every week had a Thursday. Gradually his inner security increased and he ceased to need the playroom or his friend Miss A, though he never forgot either.

Through the safety of the playroom Dibs had learned many things. "He had become a person in his own right. He had found a sense of dignity and self-respect. With this confidence and security he could learn to accept and respect other people in his world. He was no longer afraid to be himself." The playroom had been a safe place on the way to the safer place of inner security. It is vital that counselling should be safe but it must never become the goal; just a stepping stone on the way to that goal.

David was able to say to God, "You are my hiding place; You will protect me from trouble" (Ps. 32:7). Counselling should help and not hinder making this hiding place a reality for people.

A secure home is the environment that most successfully produces mature healthy adults. Children need this security if they are to develop normally and to eventually become independent. It is always interesting to see first-time parents become suddenly safety-conscious. They search out the sharp corners on which the toddler could hurt his head. They put poisons and pills out of reach; they buy guards for the fire, make gates for the stairs and so on, until at last they are satisfied the baby has the safest environment possible.

The church's counselling ministry should be organised with similar care. Some of the following suggestions may appear mundane and unimportant, but, if we are concerned to protect the whole person they are all vital. We have discovered that by allowing any of these safety measures or boundaries to lapse we jeopardise the healing process.

3

DEFINING THE LIMITS

It should be quite clear that there is a significant difference between secular counselling and that of a local church. Many of the boundaries will be relevant in both settings but owing to the family-type relationships in the local church some others must be added. The trained secular counsellor has the protection of his professionalism – an office setting, a secretary, a business phone number and an appointment system. He is unlikely to meet his client outside the counselling hour. In fact for some professionals it has been part of the contract to avoid any social contact at all. There is a privacy about this arrangement which can be very safe for both parties. None of this is possible in the local church where the type of ministry we are talking about occurs.

Most of us at some stage in our lives would probably benefit from some counselling and ministry for a variety of problems ranging from family and marriage difficulties to personality problems that inhibit and limit us. Although these may not be severe enough to ask for professional help, some help from outside the immediate family could be very beneficial.

If our churches are to become healing fellowships provision must be made for ministry to a whole spectrum of human need. Obviously in some cases it will be necessary to call on the help of a professional counsellor. Mostly, however it should be possible to meet these needs within the body of believers with the resources and gifting God has placed there.

Differences between the secular and church counselling

Distinctions between the two types of counselling fall mainly into the areas of relationships, the available resources and training.

1. Relationships in the local church

Jesus commanded His disciples to "love each other as I have loved you" (John 15:12). He prayed "that all of them may be one, Father, just as you are in me and I am in you" (John 17:21). He told them, "you also should wash one another's feet" (John 13:14). All this speaks of intimate relationships in the family of God. We are heirs together of the same Heavenly Father.

Even if a person has been set aside to counsel and minister to people regularly by the leadership of the church he is still a member of the body of Christ in that place; an ordinary person on the same road to maturity as everyone else in the church. This person may be counselling another church member on a Friday and perhaps sitting beside him in church on a Sunday. On the Friday the relationship is one of counsellor to counsellee. On the Sunday it is friend to friend. Both may also be involved in praying for the sick at the end of the service when the relationship changes yet again to one of partners.

As we grow in our understanding of the therapeutic relationship, and the feelings that can occur within it we recognise that some very real difficulties are involved here. It can be hard for people to weather the vulnerability and pain of counselling and simultaneously maintain a normal relationship with their counsellor/friend, but it is not impossible providing those difficulties are understood and catered for.

Setting limits will help to make counselling easier and build in "safety" for both counsellor and counsellee. As we shall see later, the relationship has within it the potential for healing and growth. It also has within it the seeds for misunderstanding, hurt and sad to say, immorality.

2. Resources available
The local church has much more support to offer than a secular counsellor. When a person expresses a need for help he is put in touch with a suitable person. At the same time he can be supported by understanding Christian friends in his home group or Bible-study fellowship. Personal growth courses are available in some churches which will help his understanding. And prayer is available in many church services if he is finding things particularly difficult. Such resources are not available to the secular counsellor. His resources are mostly limited to the time and expertise he can give during the counselling session, with the possibility of group therapy for some clients.

3. Training
The professional psychotherapist has a great deal of training in theory and technique to assist him, besides knowing others with similar experience and expertise to consult with.

The Christian layman works out of his natural abilities and whatever training and reading is available to him. During the ministry times he relies heavily upon the supernatural gifting and presence of the Holy Spirit to guide and heal.

However, it should be recognised that the layman has his limitations and there will be times when the person seeking help needs the expertise of a professional counsellor.

Limits around the church's counselling ministry

To make the healing process safe for all concerned, limits should be placed around the following:

1. Clientele
The local church is only responsible for facilitating the health and growth of its own membership. For reasons of

safety it is best to limit ministry to those within this local family where the ministry can be responsibly carried out. Cries for help will come from far and wide but it is impossible to monitor or support those who come from a distance.

Advice should always be sought before ministering to anyone with a history of mental illness, suicide attempts or severe depression.

2. Time

It is essential to have a set time to meet. Punctuality is very important for both counsellor and counsellee. For the counsellor to be late will give the impression that the appointment is not very significant to him and so leave the counsellee with feelings of rejection. When the counsellee is late the counsellor may be frustrated over the waste of time – especially when he has other counsellees queuing up for a time to see him.

The length of the session should be agreed upon and adhered to. Some people come purposefully into counselling determined to get to the bottom of their problems and ready to co-operate. Such are a joy to work with and make the best use of the time available. Others may have avoided facing their painful feelings all their lives and though they have chosen to come for ministry their protective habit may well cause them to use every avoidance technique they know. This very often takes the form of intellectualising about their problems. Talking about feelings rather than feeling them does not heal them. To talk about their neurosis may help a person to understand it but it does not usually cure it. It just makes the person a wiser neurotic!

A certain amount of time may be allotted to reviewing what has happened since the last appointment. If the counsellee has kept a journal anything relevant may be shared at this point. However, be aware of the clock and never let the discussion run away with the time so that no space is left for in-depth ministry. A clock in a visible place is a helpful addition to the counselling room.

The time allotted should be adhered to however slow the

beginning may have been. A counsellee will gradually learn to make the most of the session. If the time is left open and elastic the counsellee may become more and more demanding and manipulative, bringing up new problems in order to prolong the appointment. The end result will be boredom and exhaustion for the counsellor and unhelpful regression to childish behaviour for the counsellee.

It is also advisable to set some limitations on the duration of counselling to be given. To suggest four sessions might seem reasonable to start with. It is always possible to extend for a further period if good progress is being made.

In some cases the counsellee may only have asked for one interview to sort out a specific problem. Or it may be that a counsellor and counsellee have some arrangement whereby the counsellee has permission to make an appointment when a specified need arises. In this case there is an on-going counselling relationship which occurs at intervals. In a church set-up this seems to work well. These are the people who are growing as Christians and learning to deal with their own weak areas. Occasionally, however, they become stuck and need some outside help. Usually one session will sort them out. People who come into this category have usually attended a personal growth course; or received some in-depth ministry. This means they understand the counselling procedures and are extremely co-operative. They are prepared to take responsibility for their problems and the work involved in overcoming them.

Another potential difficulty is the question of how much time should be spent with a counsellee outside the counselling room discussing his problems and ministering to him. Occasions for this abound in the ordinary course of church life. There are many times when a counsellee and counsellor will be attending the same meetings when there will be opportunity for ministry or chatting. Every case is different and the counsellor has to use his judgement. The guiding principle in each situation has to be one of love. This will govern the amount of time and attention which must be given to others present. It will also raise the question of whether, "my involvement in this person's on-going problem will enhance or inhibit his spiritual and emotional growth". It is important to discuss such eventualities with the counsellee at the very beginning of counselling. It needs to be explained that there is a danger of the relationship becoming problem-centred and therefore it is healthier to keep ministry for the appointed times. However, it is possible to leave the door open for telephone contact should the feelings become too difficult to handle.

It may seem to be a loving act to offer more time and support to a troubled person. However, many Christian counsellors have started off by doing this only to find the counsellee regressing into a very dependent childish state. The whole process has consequently become very exhausting, time-consuming and non-productive as far as any kind of healing is concerned. It should be borne in mind that hurting people are nearly always manipulative either consciously or unconsciously.

Virginia Axline faces this dilemma with Dibs on his first visit. Dibs does not want to leave her and begins to cry. Again on the second session he is upset when the time comes to an end. "No," he shouted, "Dibs no go out of here, Dibs no go home. Not ever." Miss A answers him, "I know you don't want to go Dibs, but you and I only have one hour every week to spend together here in this playroom. And when that hour is over, no matter how you feel about it, no matter how I feel about it, no matter how anybody feels about it, it is over for that day and we both leave the playroom."

She then explains to the reader that "this hour was only a part of his existence, that it could not and should not take precedence over all other relationships and experience, that all the time between the weekly sessions was important too . . . If the therapy becomes the predominant and controlling influence in the individual's daily life, then I would have serious doubts as to its effectiveness".

To encourage someone to expect or hope that another person will make him feel better or resolve his problems for him is not truly loving. But to help an individual take responsibility for his own life, and to stand with God's strength on his own feet is a loving act.

So then, if the time limits are clearly set out and agreed to at the outset, many difficulties will be avoided.

3. Place

Time is an important factor; so also is the place. The place can be a help or hindrance to healing.

The best setting for counselling is a quiet private place where there is no fear of disturbing or of being disturbed by others. For added protection a "Do not disturb" notice may be hung on the door. No one is going to allow his defences to come down unless he is safe.

I remember a woman who was sitting in our secluded upper room suddenly becoming very agitated. "Shut the window," she demanded. "Please shut it!" Since it was a warm day the cold was obviously not the problem. "I don't want anyone to hear me," she whispered. Another lady became very distressed when, coming down the stairs from the upper room, she almost bumped into a cleaner. She shrank back against the wall in fear of being seen.

On one memorable occasion when I was receiving some ministry myself in a friend's house, the door bell went. I will never forget the feeling of panic that nearly engulfed me. It was as if I had unpacked all my most intimate belongings and strewn them round the room then suddenly I somehow had to push them all back into the suitcase and hide them from view.

This fear of being disturbed needs to be guarded against and the counsellee assured of complete safety for the space allotted to him.

Comfort is also important. A counsellee may writhe in emotional discomfort but not from uncomfortable seating. He may shiver from fear but not from cold. He may perspire with anxiety but not with over heating.

When a counsellee cries copiously it is yet another distraction if there are no tissues available. As feelings begin to surface a person may swallow continually trying to control the rising pain. Water needs to be on hand to relieve the dry mouth. At the beginning of counselling a person may well go through many glasses of water. As, in the process of time, they become more adept at expressing rather than suppressing feelings they will need the water less and the tissues more!

A variety of cushions on the floor will ensure the comfort of everyone should the counsellee decide to work kneeling down or lying down.

4. The relationship

As we shall see in chapter four the relationship between the counsellee and counsellor is one of the most important factors. Psychotherapists speak of a "therapeutic alliance" being made by which is meant a healing relationship, or friendship, or companionship, or better still, a partnership. For this partnership to be truly healing it also needs clearly stated limits of propriety beyond which neither party strays. We remember again that Jude exhorts his readers to stay within the boundaries where God's love can reach and bless us. The relationship can be the most dangerous area of all. It is at this point that many shipwrecks occur; therefore we must raise the warning flag energetically.

The safety of the relationship

The positive nature of this relationship will be explored later. For the present we are looking merely at the safety factor. We need first to recognise the dangers and then to build limits around them. As the counsellor is primarily responsible for the safety of the relationship the greatest danger lies within the counsellor himself.

1. Naïvety is a dangerous trait in a counsellor

The counsellor needs to be "as shrewd as snakes and as innocent as doves" (Matt. 10:16). Shrewd in understanding the fallen nature of man and innocent of involvement in any sinful deeds. Paul exhorts his readers "to be wise about what is good, and innocent about what is evil" (Rom. 16:19).

A person who is not aware of his own capacity to sin is not safe. He should not be counselling until he can acknowledge that "the heart is deceitful above all things and beyond cure" (Jer. 17:9).

2. The danger of unmet needs

Where the counsellor is unconsciously counselling to meet his own neurotic needs, such as to be needed, to be loved, or to be in control of others similar danger arises. In such cases the driving force behind the counselling will be one's own unmet needs. Everyone has some unmet basic needs. The danger is when these are not recognised. When a "rescuer" or a person with the need to direct another's life comes into contact with a counsellee who has the problem of childhood deprivation for example, the relationship can quickly flare into an alliance of a binding and unhealthy nature.

3. Ignorance of the dynamics

Another pitfall is a lack of understanding about the dynamics of the counselling relationship.

Under normal circumstances people keep safe distances between themselves and others. Their ego-boundaries are intact. In the intimacy of the counselling room these normal defences come down. The secrets of the heart are unlocked, pain surfaces and the usual controls are not functioning normally. Some very basic and primitive needs may be laid bare at that moment and expressed with urgency. A counsellor may spontaneously move in closer to comfort the counsellee without fully realising the strength of the hunger being expressed.

Leanne Payne tells of instances where a counselling situation between one woman and another has resulted in a lesbian relationship. "This can happen when the inner loneliness and tactile needs of someone (such as one suffering from infantile deprivation) come into collusion with another's need to shape, direct, 'do things to' or otherwise control and dominate another soul" (*The Broken Image*).

In the same book Leanne Payne tells the story of two attractive married women who fell separately into lesbian relationships after becoming Christians. "At the very least the kind of love got grievously mixed in their attempts to help a close friend, and each woman ended by misusing and perverting the human love in order to meet her own needs and the needs of another."

I was handed the following poem by a counsellee. It poignantly describes the hunger within the heart of so many people.

Seeking the eternal mother . . . we wander
From soul to soul, ever grasping, hoping, evading,
Desperate, yet terrified of ever finding her.
We say one thing, but our eyes display the ever
                present need.

Touching, embracing, tossing our bodies between
                shadows,
Longing through it all to find father, to at last come
                home . . .
Home from our exile in the desert of loneliness, of
                non-being . . .
We think we have finally found our reason to live –
                to love . . .

Yet the lie seeps mercilessly through our dream . . .
And once more our bodies lie discarded on the rocks.

And you, O Lord, are ever to be found waiting,
Reaching out to our battered hearts,
Longing to restore the dignity that was never ours.

You want to take us in your arms
Stroke our hair, and sing soft lullabies to us.

You want to play football, and hide and seek
You want to protect us from the big bad wolf in our
dreams.

Yet we keep running to the cheap imitations,
Suffering their limitations
Agonising through the dark and pain-ridden nights.

Come mother of my soul,
Hold me father of my life,
The child in me is calling out to you . . .
The desert must live without my presence
My captive heart must now be caught by you.

4. Faulty judgement

To dismiss these hazards as rare occurrences and being sure
of one's own strength to avoid such situations is yet another
danger. "So, if you think you are standing firm, be careful
that you don't fall!" (1 Cor. 10:12).

We have wept with pastors and leaders; broken men and
women caught up in some immoral act while counselling
desperately needy people. On the other side we have felt
the distress and disillusionment of people, who in the
process of a counselling relationship, have gone along with
improper suggestions without objecting. Not wanting to
lose the care and attention of the counsellor and still
longing to have some childhood needs met they have been
led like a lamb to the slaughter.

Safeguards

A good counselling relationship can benefit both counsellor
and counsellee in terms of growth and insight. Therefore
from the beginning precautions should be taken to protect
this relationship. The following suggestions may be helpful.

1. Supervision

This way of protecting the relationship is easily arranged in the secular world but in the local church it is difficult where confidentiality is a priority. It is, however, possible to have one of the church leaders in charge of all counselling in the church, to whom all counsellors are accountable. It is not necessary to give a detailed account of the counsellee's problem: the fact of being answerable to a supervisor is a way of controlling any excess.

2. When counselling alone

If the counsellor is ever on his own the rule should be to minister only to someone of the same sex.

3. Counselling in partnership

The best safety measure is a counselling partnership. Working in twos prevents many mistakes. The counsellees may express difficulty in relating to two people at the same time. However the benefits far outweigh what will only be an initial problem. Two people provide the checks and balances needed in the use of the gifts of the Spirit. In the case of demonic oppression there is safety and strength in two. If the counsellee needs an expression of love and support from a counsellor it is much less likely to lead on to something sexual whilst there is another person present.

Inevitably counselling carries with it special stresses and strains. To spend the day listening to, praying with and counselling hurting people can be emotionally exhausting and a heavy responsibility. It is a relief to be able to discuss openly a counselling session and plan the way ahead with another person without breaking the rule of confidentiality.

For this partnership to work well there has to be a high level of trust and compatibility. It is worth the pain of dealing immediately with any misunderstanding which may rise in order to keep the lines of communication clear.

4

THE RELATIONSHIP

> Counselling now seems to have taken the place of a cup
> of tea, a dram of brandy, shared grief, friendship,
> pastoral visitation and family life.
>
> So I was not surprised to hear, after the horror of the
> Hungerford massacre, that what the shocked villagers
> needed now was counselling. 'The social services are
> moving in,' said a reporter on BBC Radio 4, 'to offer the
> survivors counselling.'
>
> Of course people need to share grief and shock, but
> where are the churches, where are family friends? Gone
> to counsellors, every one. [Comment in the *Sunday
> Telegraph* August 23, 1987.]

The professional psychiatrists, psychotherapists, and
counsellors with their training and skill will be increasingly
in demand for the ever growing number of sick and
disorientated people being cast up on the shores of our
society today. Nevertheless, though training is always
beneficial it may not be the crucial factor in healing. Peter
Lomas in his book on *Personal Psychotherapy* suggests that
psychotherapy "is less a science than a craft, but it is a craft
the aptitude for which derives more from a personal
experience of living than is usually supposed". In another
place he says, "If we are to search for a paradigm for our
work we should look to that of friendship rather than the
application of scientific theory." And later, "I am not alone
in openly stating that the therapist's love for his patient
often plays a significant part in healing and may even be the
crucial factor."

The relationship between the client and therapist is more important in the healing process than any learned scientific theory. Peter Lomas feels that the distinction made between befriending, counselling, psychotherapy and psychoanalysis is artificial and that the only difference lies in the degree of need within the individual seeking help. He argues, "There is not necessarily any basic difference in the nature of the transaction." He goes on to describe a person with a healing attitude who can both "focus on another person in a certain situation" and also has a "capacity to foster growth" in that person. He uses words like integrity, warmth, openness, courage, sensitivity, tolerance and humility to describe such a person. He is describing a human being who seeks to help another because he has a natural aptitude for the task.

Two important factors that contribute to the healing and growth of an individual are the personality of the counsellor and the relationship or friendship that grows up between him and his client.

Another psychotherapist writes "that it had gradually been driven home to me that I cannot be of help to the troubled person by means of any intellectual or training procedures. No approach which relies upon knowledge, upon training, upon acceptance of something that is taught is of any use . . . The failure of any such approach through the intellect has forced me to recognise that change appears to come through an experience in a relationship" (*On Becoming a Person*, Carl Rogers).

Because of this potential for healing and growth in the counselling relationship it is worth spending time planning and building – in the safety measures and boundaries we described earlier. It is too valuable a tool to be carelessly treated.

What are the dynamics then of this therapeutic relationship? Professionally it is between two people but in the case of our church situation it is normally between three. There are the two helpers and one who is seeking help. The helpers must have the ability to foster growth within another person.

Requirements for a Christian counsellor

We look for all of the following qualities in a person coming forward as a counsellor:

1. An intuitive understanding of human nature
2. Good common sense
3. Experience of life
4. A high degree of interest in people generally
5. An ability to focus fully on another and enter into his world
6. A natural aptitude
7. A Holy Spirit anointing for the work

In secular counselling this last ingredient will not be considered important. However, for any ministry in the Church a special calling and anointing by the Holy Spirit should be expected. In the Acts of the Apostles we find the seven men who were set aside to wait on tables were specially chosen. "'Brothers, choose seven men from among you who are known to be full of the Spirit and wisdom. We will turn this responsibility over to them and will give our attention to prayer and the ministry of the word'". "They presented these men to the apostles, who prayed and laid their hands on them" (Acts 6:3, 4, 6). Those who are to be involved in the Church's ministry of inner healing and counselling should be equally chosen and prayed over.

Although one missing ingredient would not disqualify a person from helping another, it would disqualify him from the church counselling room. A person may be interested in people but have little understanding of human nature. The church welcoming committee may well be much more suitable for him. Someone else may have a lot of experience of life and be interested in people but lack the aptitude needed for counselling.

Attitude to counsellee

The counsellor with the required qualifications must also be prepared:

1. To be real
For the relationship to have reality the counsellor must lead the way in honestly expressing his different feelings and attitudes. The more genuine the counsellor the more likely the counsellee is to be genuine also.

2. To be warm and accepting
This means to accept every part of the counsellee; to accept his bad feelings as well as his good ones, his opinions and attitudes. Acceptance does not necessarily mean agreement.

A little while ago a young woman came to see me and told me a tragic story of teenage rebellion which led her into sexual promiscuity and one disastrous relationship after another. She was presently sleeping with her boyfriend though she had become a Christian the previous year. As I listened I was wondering if this would be the right time to comment on this present relationship and point out the biblical view of sex. I decided to say nothing and continued to listen. She described how depressed she was feeling and how much she disliked herself. Suddenly she stopped talking and looking straight at me she asked: "Does the Bible really say it's wrong to have sex outside marriage?" I replied with a murmur, "I'm afraid so." She then looked at me with real anguish, sighing deeply. "Please help me to stop," she pleaded.

My listening had been an acceptance of her as a person of worth but it did not compromise me into agreeing with what she had done and was doing. Our job is not to judge and condemn but to help people on the road to healthy maturity in Christ.

3. To show empathy

Our acceptance is not enough. Troubled people also seek our understanding of their plight. It requires an effort to get under the skin of another person, to enter his world, to see and feel it as he sees and feels it. As a counsellor does this the counsellee begins to sense the freedom and the courage to explore those hidden places within himself and may proceed to share the frightening, the miserable, the weak, the horrid and weird parts of himself with his counsellor.

"When such conditions are achieved," observes Carl Rogers, "I become a companion to my client accompanying him in the frightening search for himself which he now feels free to undertake" (*On Becoming a Person*).

Ingredients in the relationship

Largely the initiative for forming this healing relationship falls on the shoulders of the counsellor or therapist. However for such a relationship to produce fruit certain ingredients will have to be present.

1. Compatibility

This relationship has been likened to friendship. For friendship to exist two people must like one another's company, want to be together and have something in common. For counselling to be effective liking is necessary, mutual respect should exist and there should be a looking forward to coming together each week.

Every Friday I counsel all day with the wife of another member of staff. Sometimes we have been asked to see complex and difficult cases. It is a long hard day and yet I always wake up with anticipation on those days. Counsellees who come regularly to see us have become friends and we look forward to that time with them. They are often deeply troubled and their pain can be heart-rending. Nevertheless we come each week wanting to stand with them, fight with them, share with them in their struggles and pray with them. We are continually moved by their courage and desire to be whole.

In contrast I had occasion to see a single woman with rather unspecific problems. She had never been happy and had once vaguely attempted suicide. Whenever the appointment time came, I anticipated it with a feeling of heaviness. I always felt slightly bored and was quite unable to enter her world. After several months we drew to a halt. Superficially she had appeared to make progress but I suspected her heart was not in changing and growing, so much as in being supported by someone older than herself. I could sympathise with this desire but felt quite unable to make a relationship that would be really helpful to her. On reflection I realise that we lacked the ingredient of compatibility.

The journey into a "fully human, fully alive" existence requires certain supplies and provisions. John Powell in his book of that title lists amongst such requirements "a friend confidant. A person with whom we can be totally open is for many reasons an absolute requirement for growth into fullness of life."

Compatibility is essential then if a healing relationship is to develop.

2. Safety
The limits we place around counselling will help provide this. However, if the counsellee is to be able to explore and express his painful feelings he needs to feel totally safe to do so. This must be both within the boundaries we have already described and with the friendship and acceptance of his counsellor. He needs to know that whatever he expresses he will not be rejected. Nor will it be repeated outside the counselling room. This is particularly important in the local church where a break in confidentiality could have disastrous effects.

3. Tenacity
The ability of a counsellor or counsellee to "hang in there" will carry him through the sticky patches. This quality will

be especially required if the relationship is threatened by the counsellee becoming very dependent on the counsellor or by a counsellee transferring feelings applicable to another significant person, on to the counsellor. In the course of counselling this is almost unavoidable and if not properly understood can cause bewilderment and anxiety. Tenacity will ensure that both counsellor and counsellee ride the storm.

In psychoanalysis transference is analysed and becomes a part of the therapeutic process. Certainly when it happens it is best to bring it out into the open and work with the feelings that have surfaced. In the process of experiencing the feelings they will be transferred back and connected to their original cause. With appropriate ministry at this point insight as well as healing will result.

Some time ago I spent time counselling a woman who went through a patch of feeling very dependent upon me. She bravely brought it out into the open and we were able to talk about it. It did not worry me unduly as I felt sure she would work through it. Despite all my assurances this friend was very thrown by the feelings. Recently we were chatting over coffee and discussing the counselling experience we had shared together. She told me with feeling, "That awful dependency was the worst of all. It really frightened me!"

Transference, dependency, regression to childish behaviour are all similar experiences which we will discuss in chapter five. These can be very difficult for both counsellor and counsellee. However the next ingredient in the relationship can make this a positive rather than a negative experience.

4. Openness and honesty

The contract between counsellor and counsellee should include this requirement. Without such openness there will always be "hidden agendas" – unspoken expectations which have been frustrated or disappointed. Very little progress will be made where thoughts and feelings of this kind have to be concealed.

At some point in the relationship, preferably early, a firm resolution to work at honest communication must be made. John Powell says that this must be a "flint hard posture of the will", whereby we make a promise to work at it. "This commitment is unconditional: no fine print in the contract, no 'ifs' or 'buts' or time limits. I will work at it when it is easy and when it is difficult. I will try to tell you who I am. And I will listen to learn who you are . . . Together we will work at sharing until we have built strong lines of communication. Only then can we experience the personal fulfilment that comes with effective communication" (*Will the Real Me Please Stand Up*).

Sometimes the feelings expressed by a counsellee are not ones of transference. He may genuinely have a problem handling some behaviour quirk or personal mannerism of the counsellor. If these difficulties remain unspoken they will block the healing and the relationship ceases to be therapeutic.

So much for the healing relationship and the boundaries surrounding it. Now we will turn our attention to some common phenomena that often occur during the process of counselling. These could be either stepping stones or stumbling blocks to healing.

5

STEPPING STONES OR STUMBLING BLOCKS

(Regression, Dependency and Transference)

As we have explained already the relationship between counsellee and counsellor has within it the capacity to harm as well as to heal. We have seen that misunderstanding the dynamics of this relationship can be a potential danger in counselling. In order to give a greater degree of under-standing and to open up the possibilities we will highlight several of the common phenomena which could occur during counselling. These could cause a counsellee to stumble or may become a stepping stone on the road to healing.

Regression

This is defined as a return to childish behaviour which, in normal circumstances, would be seen as unacceptable.

Unconscious regression

There seem to be various types of regression which we meet in the process of counselling. The first is an unconscious regression. The counsellee returns to being dependent and childish without any realisation of what is happening. Constant demands are made on the counsellor for care and support. There is no sense of responsibility for self or concern for others. The craving for love and support is all consuming. A friend recently told me of a counsellee who would not leave once her session had ended; instead she clung to her counsellor demanding more time. The fact that another person was waiting outside and losing time made no impact. Eventually my friend decided to treat the counsellee as she would a small child. She told her firmly that every time she made a fuss about leaving their following appointment would be cancelled. This resolved the immediate problem, though I believe the young woman continued to regress in other ways and made very little progress.

Not many counsellors in a church environment could cope with this kind of a situation. They would soon be overwhelmed and such constant demands would be emotionally draining. This form of regression is not usually a very healing experience, containing as it does more destructive than constructive elements. It could take years to work through this type of regression but it might be possible if someone, who has a great deal of patience and very few other responsibilities, were to take on the mothering.

"From the earliest days of psychoanalysis it has been known that under certain conditions patients may enter upon a form of regression, to a primitive state in which they make increasing demands for attention and gratification which can never be satisfied. This process is not readily reversible, and the possibilities for a creative outcome are more uncertain" (*The Dynamics of Religion*, Bruce Reed). It would seem then that the condition may point to a greater degree of sickness than most laymen could easily cope with.

Temporary regression

The next form of regression is of a temporary nature. It occurs when a person cannot find the resources within himself to face a difficult situation. At that moment the person becomes childish and resorts to an infantile mode of behaviour.

I remember such a situation myself when I was eight

months' pregnant with our fourth baby. David announced, one evening, that he had been asked to go to Australia for a month's deputation work under the missionary society we worked with. It would mean his leaving two weeks after the new baby was born. I remember crying like a child and begging him not to leave me. At that moment I felt as if I had no resources to help me cope in such an eventuality. My "adult" flew out of the window and the "child" took over. Fortunately it was only a temporary regression from which I soon recovered! Kind friends rallied round to support me and David was able to go.

Crisis counselling is usually involved with helping someone to deal with circumstances in which they feel unable to cope and so become helpless. For a time they become dependent upon someone who seems stronger. This sort of regression does not last and can be a point of growth if the sufferer is enabled to gain some inner strength and grow a little in maturity through it. It can also be used for gaining insight into the weak and hurting part within; to receive healing for those hurts that have become sensitised by the crisis.

Creative regression

The third form of regression is creative regression. This is recognised by both counsellor and counsellee and is used for the purposes of healing. During the sessions together in the "safe place", the counsellee is given permission to explore the variety of childish feelings being stimulated by memories from the past, by present-day happenings and even by the counselling relationship.

In psychotherapy the facilitating environment "is provided by the physical setting, and by the attention, understanding and security conveyed by the therapist" (*The Dynamics of Religion*, Bruce Reed).

A counsellee should be encouraged to explore the needy feelings that start to surface and then to express them aloud. In so doing, what may start, for example, as present feelings of need for care from the counsellor, may quickly connect up to the past feelings of need for Mummy's love and support. Quite often the regression becomes a reliving of a traumatic event of childhood deprivation or abuse. On one occasion as I drew my chair towards a counsellee to pray she moved instinctively away from me. I encouraged her to explore the feelings that my movement towards her had stimulated. She then began to describe the feelings being aroused by my closeness. Quite quickly she moved from a rational description of feelings into an emotional expression of fear and panic caused by being in close proximity to an abusive parent.

"Regression may facilitate more vivid uncovering and exploration by helping clients to loosen habitual patterns of control. Regression is an important ingredient in most long-term therapies and it can be enhanced in cathartic therapy" (*Emotional Expression in Psychotherapy*, Pierce, Nichols and DuBrin).

The writers of the above book go on to talk of this regression as being a "bridge to the past". In this "creative regression" feelings are put squarely where they belong. Instead of anger or need being directed at the counsellor the feelings are connected to their original cause. The counsellee comes out of such an experience having gained insight, understanding and, where needed, has released forgiveness to the person who caused the original hurt. Whereas at the beginning of the session the childish feelings seemed to be a painful and embarrassing stumbling block, once connected to the source they become stepping stones to be employed usefully in the process of healing.

Dependency

As we have already seen, this aspect of regression is almost an occupational hazard. Many secular therapists would be very careful not to encourage dependency. "They do little to help, support, or care for the client, instead presenting themselves as strictly neutral. These therapists are concerned that more nurturant behaviour would be a disservice to the client as it would encourage harmful, unrealistic dependency" (*Emotional Expression in Psychotherapy*, Pierce, Nichols and DuBrin).

Such cold, distant, relationships are impossible in the loving supportive environment of the Christian family. Therefore we will almost certainly have to face the issue of dependency sooner or later.

The major problem here is one of motivation. A counsellee who finds love and support within the counselling relationship may for a time lose his desire to be healed. It is so good being cared for that the thought of being well and losing such special treatment is unacceptable.

On the positive side, however, these dependent feelings can be used in the therapeutic process. They afford the counsellee the opportunity to work through unresolved problems with past care givers who have either not been sufficiently supportive or have over-protected and not encouraged independence. This need to be dependent may go back to difficulties in separating from mother during the first year of life. At about seven months a baby begins to realise his own identity apart from his mother. It is at this point he needs help coping with the dilemma of his desire for both attachment and separation. During this stage the baby will often attach to a transitional object like a stuffed rabbit on to which emotions are transferred from the mother. This helps him start the separation process. John Cleese and Robin Skynner discuss this process in their book *Families and How to Survive Them*:

"The fact that the mother approves of the baby playing with the rabbit carries the message that it's good for the baby to become more independent. In other words, this rabbit is a memory-mother, an edge-clarifier, a teacher of self-mothering and an independence-approver."

Sometimes, however, this process is complicated because the mother hinders the baby in his attempts at separation because of her own problems. As a result the baby is being denied support from his mother whilst at the same time he is conscious of his mother's need for love from him. "So even if she does give him a rabbit, it won't have the right message with it. So both ways the baby is failing to get the confidence he needs to let go and move on. So he's bound to finish up 'stuck', clinging, unable to become more independent of Mother. He's on the unhealthy track and more likely to grow into an adult who suffers from a depressive illness" (*Families and How to Survive Them*, John Cleese and Robin Skynner).

The way through the problem of dependency is along the pathways of truth, support and work.

Truth
Part of the contract between counsellor and counsellee should be of openness and truth. The possibility of dependency needs to be faced and understood. It should be made clear to the counsellee how this would be handled. He needs to know that, though painful, these feelings are normal and not sinful. One young woman told me she suffered from bad feelings of guilt when she became very attached to and dependent upon her counsellor. She feared she was beginning to "worship" her counsellor and thus sinning and becoming idolatrous!

Support
If the counsellee is to work through any unfinished process of attachment and separation he needs the right kind of support. The counsellor must be prepared to do what mother did not do, which is to give the opportunity for the counsellee first to attach and then to begin gradually to separate. To begin with there will be some oscillation. Attaching then separating; attaching then separating. At first for short times, then for longer until independence is achieved. We see this oscillation with toddlers at play. For a while they run and play and then suddenly, as if to reassure themselves, they rush back to mother. Just as suddenly off they go again. Backwards and forwards they

go wavering between separation and attachment. As he grows bigger the toddler gets braver and spends more time playing away from Mummy. The end result is separation and independence, unless the process is interrupted as happened to my three-year-old grandson while on holiday recently. He was playing on the beach a little way from his mother. All of a sudden a big dog came bouncing up wanting to join in Timmy's game. Tim screamed with fear which excited the dog even more, causing him to jump up and put his huge paws on Tim's little shoulders. By the time he was rescued he was shaking with fear. For the rest of the holiday he was more preoccupied with attachment than separation!

Oscillation occurs too in counselling. Often some very sticky patches arise when a counsellee is frightened by something and the whole counselling process stands still; even appears to regress. One of the keys is knowing when to give support and when to allow the counsellee to feel and experience his own strength simultaneously encouraging him to go through a degree of separation.

Torey Hayden, in her book *One Child* describes this phase of attachment through which most of the children in her class passed. One of her pupils, Sheila, is no exception. She was a very damaged, abused and neglected little girl and during the year in Torey's class worked through the experience of emotional dependency upon Torey to a place of being able to leave the special class for disturbed children and enter a normal classroom. Torey describes the experience:

The first weeks she followed me around all day long. Everywhere I went, when I turned around there she would be, clutching a book to her chest or a box of maths cubes. A silly smile would spill over her lips when she caught my eye, and she'd scuttle up ready to share. I had to divide my time equally with the other children, of course, but this did not deter her. She would stand patiently behind me waiting until I had finished.

Sometimes I would feel a hand tentatively take hold of my belt as she got braver and longed for more physical contact.

Later in the year Torey speaks of the gradual separation that was taking place:

Sheila was beginning to grow away from needing to follow me around all day long. She still watched me often and would sit nearby if given a choice, but she did not need physical contact all the time. On bad days when things had gone wrong before she came to school or when the other kids gave her a hard time, or even when I reprimanded her, it was not unusual to feel her hand go through my belt and for a while once more, she would move around the room with me while I worked. I did not discourage it; I felt she needed the security of knowing I was not going to leave her. The line was fine between dependence and overdependence, but I noticed that most of my kids went through a period of intense involvement and attachment in the beginning. It seemed to be a natural phase and if things progressed right, the child outgrew the behaviour, becoming secure enough in his relationships that he no longer needed such tangible evidence of caring. So it was with Sheila.

At the end of the book Torey writes of Sheila's excitement at meeting her new teacher. "It was a sweet, sad moment for me because I knew that I had been outgrown."

So will a counsellee outgrow his need for attachment to his counsellor if given the right support while working through his difficulties.

Work
The pathway to maturity is not an easy one. It will be especially difficult for those who have experienced the deprivation of normal parenting. Sheila, aged six, worked through many of her problems during the year with Torey but she was only six and still in the process of being

moulded. Nothing was totally fixed within her as yet. It was as if her personality was still soft and pliable. Once the process started she began to change rapidly. For a counsellee who enters counselling for the first time at forty the story may be a little different. Only patient hard work will bring about the desired change in thinking and reacting which have been embedded like tram lines in the personality.

Transference

Regression into a state of dependency is probably the most common problem to overcome in the counselling relationship. However, transference may also arise and confront the counsellor and counsellee. Nevertheless it will become a stumbling block and a point of resistance only if not understood and dealt with appropriately.

The following definition may be helpful in understanding transference. It is "the displacement of feeling from one object or person to another, and particularly the process by which the patient shifts feelings and attitudes primarily applicable to parents or other significant persons, onto the analyst, or onto others who evoke similar associations. These feelings of transference are either positive (i.e. of love, trust, and expectation of kindness) or negative (i.e. of hate, distrust, or expectation of unkindness or hostility)" (*Clinical Theology*, Frank Lake). Such transference reactions occur whenever a relationship of trust is established, where the dependent person brings into the relationship a backlog of unsolved personal problems, even extending back to infancy, which have derived from parent-child interactions.

Transference can often be recognised by the element of surprise felt by the counsellor to a remark the counsellee makes about their relationship. A young woman once commented that she was disappointed because of the lack of support I gave her during sessions. Though surprised I tried to be open to any possible truth in the accusation.

After some heart-searching I had to conclude that in this instance the cap did not fit, so my job was to find out who in fact it did fit. As the session progressed it became more and more obvious that my counsellee had been very disappointed and hurt by her mother. By the end of the session it had become clear at whose door the responsibility for the disappointment lay. This incident clarified for me the particular problem that the counsellee needed to work on.

Transference can become a stumbling block for both counsellee and counsellor wherever there is a failure to recognise it for what it is and to deal with it honestly. At the beginning of the relationship the more positive feelings may be expressed. As the counselling progresses the angrier feelings will probably begin to surface. These are frequently directed at the counsellor. When they remain unspoken the session will become bogged down with too much "hidden agenda". No progress will be made unless this is brought out into the open and expressed.

The difficulties mentioned so far have to do mainly with the relationship of the counsellee with his counsellor. We shall now move on to some other problems that are frequently encountered in counselling and could easily become stumbling blocks for all concerned.

6

FURTHER STEPPING STONES OR STUMBLING BLOCKS

Even though counselling may start with the counsellee expressing a desire to change, agreeing to co-operate and to work towards certain goals, stumbling blocks may soon appear to counter this change. One such stumbling block is "resistance".

Resistance

This is a protective device which comes into operation automatically but quite unconsciously whenever a person is threatened. This is inevitable; particularly as the counsellee begins to experience those long-avoided painful feelings, or as he tries to experiment with new behaviour patterns.

One counsellee we worked with made steady progress, facing up to traumatic incidents in her childhood – incidents which had had many repercussions during her lifetime. She bravely faced the buried memories and expressed many of the feelings she had repressed. But when it came to the point of actually trying to change some of the neurotic behaviour patterns that had resulted from the childhood abuse, the progress plateaued. For weeks we were at a standstill. Every suggestion was resisted or in some way avoided. At this point we had to stop and talk through the problem and decide how best to continue. It is here that we see the importance of the initial agreement to which we can draw the counsellee's attention.

That agreement was made with the "adult" part of the counsellee; the part that actually wants to change and not with the fearful "child within" who long ago made a decision to protect himself at all costs.

Progress will continue only if the counsellee is prepared to recognise the existence of resistance. He should then take responsibility for it and agree to work hard in partnership with his counsellor to find a way through the impasse. If this proves too difficult and the stalemate continues it may be best to discontinue counselling for a while. The counsellee can always come back at a later date if he would like to try once more to overcome the difficulty. With experience a counsellor can grow in his ability to deal with such challenges. But even the most experienced may sometimes fail to overcome this particular kind of stumbling block.

Repetition

Many of the books on "Inner Healing" or "Healing of Memories" give the impression that any hurt or trauma brought to the surface by God and ministered to once will be automatically healed and finished with. It may then come as an uncomfortable surprise if it surfaces once again. "But I thought that was all healed" is a common cry.

Before a person can actually let go of a past trauma which has given rise to wrong attitudes and neurotic behaviour he may need to return to the event several times both verbally and emotionally. He may have to talk about it from other angles and perhaps experience the full variety of feelings that each memory evokes. He may have to release forgiveness again and again till it really comes "from the heart" (Matt. 18:35). Patiently the counsellor needs to allow this process to be repeated until every aspect has been exhausted and the wound drained dry. Only then is the counsellee free to leave it behind. Occasionally thereafter he may recall it with some sadness, but as one who visits the grave of a buried relative.

It was interesting to read in *One Child* how Sheila needed to go over and over certain experiences. When her teacher, Torey Haden, was away from the class for two days, Sheila regressed into the angry unmanageable child of previous months. On Torey's return Sheila wouldn't speak to her. Torey became annoyed and there was an angry exchange between them. The incident had to be repeated over and over again by Sheila. The absence of Torey, her coming back, the angry words between them and the happy ending. There seemed to be something therapeutic in this obsessional repetition.

A septic wound cannot heal until it has been thoroughly drained of all poison. When I was little I squashed my finger in a door and it became badly infected. Twice a day I had to soak it in hot water to "draw the poison off". Every day I attended the clinic to have it dressed and receive an injection. It took several weeks to cleanse the wound enough for it to start healing. It was months before the new skin grew and years before I actually learned to use the finger again.

In one counselling situation it took several months even to open up an infected trauma. A young girl had successfully buried the memory of being assaulted and had no idea why in certain situations she reacted with such fear. Repeatedly the Holy Spirit was invited to uncover the source of the fear. Once this was accomplished the trauma then had to be drained of infection. The counsellee was encouraged week after week to express the bad feelings of fear and anger until forgiveness was fully and finally released bringing closure to the wound.

Living as we do in a local church situation we are able to monitor closely the results of ministry in people's lives. Some have experienced quick and thorough emotional healing, for which we praise God. Others spend months, even years struggling towards it. For those whose pain has affected their lives in such a way as to produce an abnormal and neurotic lifestyle, it seems to take longer to experience healing and change. It's the difference between major surgery and a minor operation.

I personally have experienced many minor inner healings of different kinds for which I thank God. But when it came to actually changing some unhealthy behaviour patterns I found that time was needed. Those wrong attitudes and reactions had formed over a lifetime. They had protected me in many ways and seemed more normal than the new ones I was trying to adopt.

Three years ago I was challenged to look again at John 17:21–23. There Jesus prays for His disciples that they may be one. I argued that some people were naturally "people people" but that I was not one of them. I liked my own company. I didn't need people that much. Slightly distant relationships suited me better than close ones. However, it was hard to ignore such words as "love one another", and "be one as I and my Father are one". But try as I might closeness produced anxiety and tension within me. I was a good listener and when focusing on others was relaxed and clear-headed, but giving away anything about myself was worse than drawing teeth. It has taken some painful hours to uncover the reasons for that anxiety and to work through it into something more akin to real Christian relationships.

As John Powell says, "There is no painless entrance into a new and fully human life." Indeed is this not part of the cross Jesus said His disciples must take up? Character and personality change takes time and hard work. Many people, who agree with the goal of maturity and wholeness often stick at superficial change.

God is able sovereignly and swiftly to penetrate the unconscious levels of our personality without any psychotherapeutic techniques. He can raise a buried trauma in one session. Even so it may still take time for it to be healed and for the healing to effect radical change in a person's way of life. Perhaps Paul was thinking along these lines when he addressed the Galatians: "My dear children, for whom I am again in the pains of childbirth until Christ be formed in you" (Gal.4:19). He regards them as immature children over whom he agonises until there is real character change and growth into the likeness of Christ.

Change takes time and may involve the counsellee in repetition and perhaps oscillation.

Oscillation

A dictionary definition of this is: "To swing to and fro like a pendulum. To vary between extremes of opinion, action" (*Chambers Everyday Dictionary*).

Changing the patterns of a lifetime can be frightening. However limiting they may be they are at least predictable and known. To change is to enter the land of the unknown. Therefore to begin with the counsellee may oscillate between the old and the new. There is an uncomfortable intermediary stage when the old doesn't fit any longer but neither does the new and so he stands in a kind of no-man's land for a while. He oscillates between trying to operate old patterns and finding them outworn and then trying to put into practice new ones and feeling himself unsure.

When I first became aware of my lack of closeness to members of the body of Christ I made a decision to change. At first every move towards closeness made me feel awkward and embarrassed. It was as if I was doing something wrong. So back I would go into my old way of relating. But that too made me feel uneasy. It was a time of chaos and took some persistence on my part, and support and encouragement from those who knew of my struggles, to make any real headway.

We have already spoken of the oscillation of the child as he seeks to find independence from Mummy. This will often be mirrored in the counselling relationship. With patience and understanding the swing of the pendulum will become less and less, until the relationship normalises and the new growth and change has become a solid reality for the counsellee.

Concluding

The last stepping stone in counselling is of course its conclusion.

There are two main reasons for ending a counselling relationship. The first reason is success in obtaining the goals set down at the outset when the counsellee is improving to such an extent that counselling is becoming unnecessary. The second is failure to alleviate symptoms or to obtain any real change in a counsellee's way of feeling, thinking and behaving. Whatever the reason for failure a conclusion is never easy and needs to be executed with care. It is always difficult to admit to failure and it is tempting for both counsellee and counsellor to blame the other for the apparent lack of success.

For the counsellor the subtle temptation is to leave the counsellee with a hint of accusation such as, "You haven't worked hard enough", or, "You don't really want to change." For the counsellee the temptation is to take the termination as "yet another rejection" and to leave feeling angry and let down.

How these stumbling blocks can be avoided

A. By booking a counsellee in for only a limited number of appointments at the beginning. For example if six is the number agreed to then at the end of the fourth session a counsellor can remind the counsellee that they only have another two to go. If after the six meetings are completed the counsellee has made very little or no progress at all, it is easier to stop then without too much trauma.

B. By admitting to being sorry that more progress has not been made and giving the counsellee permission to ask for help elsewhere should he so desire.

Just recently I heard of a counsellee who made no progress with his first counsellor and through a change of counsellor appears to have made some real headway. On the other hand the counsellor who had apparently failed was at the same time seeing progress with a young man who had previously seen at least three other counsellors without success. Sometimes, through no one's fault, it is not possible to achieve a healing relationship. There may be something in the chemistry mix with the different personalities involved. I know from my own experience that I work better with some counsellees than others just as I do with some co-counsellors.

C.   By suggesting alternatives to the counsellee. Sometimes it is obvious after a few sessions that the person is in need of professional help. Another person may be very defensive and could do better in group therapy. Information about such groups can be obtained from The London Centre for Psychotherapy. When marital problems are the constant focus of a counsellee's attention marriage counselling could be suggested and advice given as to where this help could be found.

Drawing a counselling relationship to a close can be a bitter-sweet experience. Bitter because it is the end of the intimacy of the safe place where a counsellee has had permission "to be himself" perhaps for the first time ever; where the love and acceptance has been unconditional; where it has been possible to explore what at first were frightening aspects of his personality and discover them to be acceptable. Concluding can also be sweet because a counsellee feels he is in the process of emerging, as never before, as a whole and integrated person, able to take the hand of God and face the world.

Ending counselling can be a stumbling block if done carelessly and abruptly but a stepping stone if used as a part of the counselling process and not hurried or cut short. The problem does not occur in short-term counselling, but in the case of long-term counselling it can be a painful experience.

The following report from one of our counsellors illustrates how the counselling was brought to a good conclusion:

After seeing R for over three years and having had a few 'natural breaks' such as 'faith-sharing' visits away and holidays, I was beginning to feel that R was managing to cope on her own. She had become more out-going; was well supported by her home-group, various women's groups and was helping in a number of activities within the church.

Her biggest anxiety had been faced and worked through. Almost immediately it had been put to the test and much to her surprise she had coped and not responded with her usual 'flight' pattern.

I suggested she might like to extend the time between sessions to once every two weeks, adding that her space would not be filled should she feel she needed it. At first she didn't manage the two week break but after a while she suggested herself that she would like to try again. We saw each other every two weeks over a period of two months and then R said she didn't feel she needed to come any more. I still offered her her usual space should she need it and this helped her to feel secure and able to come back at any time.

She actually has not needed to come back. I see her every Sunday and sometimes mid-week. We usually greet each other and have a chat. She sometimes asks me to pray with her in church and that seems to be enough to deal with the problems as they arise. We also minister together fairly frequently. She knows I am still there for her!

Some helpful pointers arise from this report.

a The counsellor was alert to indications that the counsellee was improving to the point of not needing the weekly sessions.

b The counsellor suggested less frequent sessions but did not insist until the counsellee felt ready for this step.

c The counsellee made the final decision to stop.

    d The counsellor assured the counsellee that she would still be there for her and that the space would not be filled immediately.

    e Counsellor and counsellee continued to have an on-going relationship on an adult level.

In the final chapter we will discuss how to recognise the signs that the counselling relationship is reaching a conclusion.

Apparent stumbling blocks can be used and turned into stepping stones in the process of counselling. Nothing need be wasted. "One of the cardinal principles of Christian pastoral counselling is that 'everything is usable'" (*Tight Corners in Pastoral Counselling*, Frank Lake).

With this in mind we will go on to explore the use of touch during counselling.

7

TO TOUCH OR NOT TO TOUCH

In my first book I wrote: "Too much touching and holding during ministry can check the work of the Spirit. Love does not mean effusive sympathy." (*Set My People Free* page 53.) Though still basically in agreement with this I would like to qualify and enlarge on it.

Over the past few years God has brought a significant increase of healing and freedom into my own life. As this has been happening I've learned to appreciate the love of the family of God expressed not only in word and deed but also in touch.

God is ultimately the only source of healing (Exodus 15:26) but He mediates that healing through us to a hurting world. The problem, as we have already seen, lies in our fallen nature and our human bias towards sin. We are all victims of "the fall" which has resulted in our being born with basic unmet needs for self-worth, security and significance. Our bias towards sin inclines us towards meeting these needs inappropriately. Hence the need for safety measures that will protect our relationships.

I remember a few years ago seeing a fascinating TV programme which demonstrated the significance of touch in the life of monkeys. Some baby monkeys were brought up normally in every way except that they were separated from their mothers by a glass wall. This enabled the babies to see and hear their mother but not touch her in any way. The result was pathetic. The babies sat forlorn in a foetal position.

Tactile starvation is a common syndrome in today's

world. Especially in the years around the war mothers were warned against picking up their babies too much. "Don't spoil them, let them cry it out," was the injunction. So in the pram and down to the bottom of the garden went the baby to endure the four lonely hours between feeds on his own – sometimes very noisily!

Ashley Montagu in his interesting and well documented book *Touching* quotes from John Broadus Watson, an influential American psychologist of the 1920s. "There is", Watson wrote, "a sensible way of treating children . . . Never hug and kiss them, never let them sit in your lap. If you must, kiss them once on the forehead when they say good night. Shake hands with them in the morning. Give them a pat on the head if they have made an extraordinary good job of a difficult task. Try it out. In a week's time you will find how easy it is to be perfectly objective with your child and at the same time kindly. You will be utterly ashamed of the mawkish, sentimental way you have been handling it" (*Psychological Care of Infant and Child*). As Ashley Montagu points out, many good mothers cried along with their babies, bravely resisting the impulse to pick them up and obediently following the advice of those in authority.

An anguished mother poignantly recalled those days in the following verses:

> They told me babies should not be held;
> It would spoil them and make them cry.
> I wished to do what is best for them,
> And the years went swiftly by.
> Now empty are my yearning arms;
> No more that thrill sublime.
> If I had my babies back again,
> I'd hold them all the time!

In more recent years procedures in the maternity units have changed. Babies are given to mothers to hold even before the cord is cut. They are left during the day to sleep alongside of mother and allowed to be fed at irregular hours if necessary. Recently my youngest daughter told me how she was massaging her tiny two-week-old son with oil and I appreciated profoundly the good she was doing. "Stroking or repetitive bodily contact is essential to his [the baby's] survival. Without it he will die, if not physically then psychologically." (*I'm OK – You're OK*, T A Harris). Later on, this need for closeness requires our hugging and kissing and caressing one another. We all need physical contact of this kind throughout life. Janov points out helpfully that "the greatest area of [our] sensory brain deals with touch; it is supremely important" (*Prisoners of Pain*).

Understanding this starvation for touch that exists within many people, and realising the dangers that this could create within the Christian family and particularly in a counselling situation, the question we must ask is: How can this need for touch be met and healed up safely?

Touching and holding in church

In the formal setting of the communion service place has been given in many churches for passing the peace to one another. This involves an embrace or handshake. It seems to be very beneficial where there exists an openness to receiving love and affection. Unfortunately some people who have not received enough physical loving as babies and toddlers have made a sort of inner vow, "It's not available for me so I won't want it – I won't even like it." So for many, passing the peace is just something to be endured and executed as quickly as possible. They draw back from such closeness and cannot receive its healing benefits.

Once the decision is made to push through the defences and protective barriers and to receive and give love, the gift of touch can be utilised at other more informal occasions. Just the other day at the end of a service in church a woman came up to me looking rather downcast. "Oh Mary", she said, "I feel very wobbly, I need a hug." I sat down and took her in my arms. I held her but said nothing. She began to cry and pour out the fears of the future that were disturbing her. She spent perhaps ten minutes in my arms at the end of which she gave a big sigh and drew away from me. "My, but that was good; I feel lots better." She looked quite different. She was more relaxed and there was a lightness about her. That hug probably did more good than an hour of just talking about her problems. Interestingly, though I was on the giving end of the hugging, I felt as if I had received as much as I had given. I too felt better for the encounter.

John Cleese continuing his discussion with Robin Skynner asks about love.

John   You know, there's one last question I want to ask. We've talked about emotional support, affection, care, love, attention, we've called it everything except mystery ingredient X. Doctor. What is this thing called 'love'?

Robin What do you think 'love' is?

John   Neatly turned . . . well, in the sense of emotional support, it's certainly partly to do with the physical act of touching. Handling, stroking, embracing, everything they used to call 'gentling'. If you're stressed, all these things make you feel better, more relaxed, give you a sense of inner calmness. They seem to help you to get things in perspective.

[*Families and How to Survive Them*]

When I was still struggling with my difficulties surrounding the area of touch, and trying to love people but still at a distance, a friend gave me a delightful little book to read called *The Little Book of Hugs* by Kathleen Keating. In it she speaks of the importance of touch. "Touch is not only nice, it's needed. Scientific research supports the theory that stimulation by touch is absolutely necessary for our physical as well as our emotional well-being."

If the Church family is to be the healing place we believe it should be, then it must be demonstrably supportive in word, deed and touch.

Touching and holding during counselling

As we examine the place of touch in the counselling relationship we do so bearing in mind the boundaries and safety measures already discussed. With a clear understanding of the dangers involved we will approach the relationship with care, "praying at all times".

At some point in nearly every interview I pray earnestly whether it is right to "touch or not to touch" to "hold or not to hold". I do not in any way want to hinder a person's struggle towards maturity and wholeness. Nor do I want to withhold support that could assist the process.

There are four major reasons for touching or holding during counselling.

To give support
When a counsellee begins to get in touch with very painful feelings, they may rise to the surface with frightening force. On occasions I have had to take a counsellee quickly into my arms and say: "It's OK you aren't going to disintegrate; just let the feelings come." One person always started hyperventilating the moment a bad memory surfaced. The only way to stop this was repeatedly to take her in my arms and say: "Push the feelings outward – cry, scream, don't draw them back down." Eventually she learned to cry and stopped the hyperventilating.

Often the only way a counsellee can actually feel safe enough to begin to explore his difficult feelings is when he is securely held.

Always after the listening part of the interview I will suggest we pray. At this point my partner and I will move our chairs closer. One of us will just lightly put one hand on the counsellee's arm or shoulder. This expresses support and togetherness. Frank Lake writes about the support needed to encourage a counsellee to make the difficult but therapeutic journey to the trapped "child" within.

> We do not run away from cries for help from babies and children. Or do we? This therapeutic journey is to hear, go to, be with, and within, to feel with and help that small person to bear and express that pain. Being encouraged to do this, and finding it shared with love, casts out the fear of it. The terrified child from which the adult had been in flight, feels itself calmed and cared for.
> [*Tight Corners in Pastoral Counselling*]

To aid diagnosis

Touch can also provide information as to the emotional state of the counsellee. Sometimes I have laid my hand gently on the arm of a counsellee only to have him jump as if shot. At that moment the most available feelings were anxiety and fear and may indicate the direction the ministry should take.

Holding a hand can convey a great deal about the counsellee. A constantly cold hand could indicate frozen feelings or submerged fear. Sweating hands may indicate nervousness. Hands that gradually increase their activity can indicate rising tension or surfacing pain. A strong grip from a counsellee conveys the understanding that this counsellee can and wants to receive support and means business.

To trigger feelings

A counsellee who finds it hard to express any feelings may do so the moment he is touched. The tenderness and empathy breaks through the defences and a torrent of feelings may be released.

To comfort

A counsellee may experience a lot of pain during a session and be emotionally taken apart. At the end of such a session he is exhausted and the memory of those painful feelings will still linger. In this case it is good to hold such a person for a time, just letting him relax and feel loved; praying quietly and letting the love of God flow gently through the counsellor to the counsellee.

Warnings

It is impossible to stress enough the danger of counselling *alone* with a member of the opposite sex. If it should ever accidently occur then holding and touching should be considered out of bounds for that time.

Even in the healthiest environment touching and holding can hold up healing if done at the wrong time and for the wrong reasons. Too much support or sympathy could keep a person in a dependent place unnecessarily. It may also prevent a person ever getting in touch with his painful feelings. For example, if the counsellee is beginning to feel some lonely feelings and starts to cry a little, to move in close and comfort at that point could thwart the full expression of the inner loneliness that was just beginning to surface and be felt.

Holding and touching when done with care and sensitivity, can be a powerful tool in the healing process. It can facilitate the release of those long suppressed healing tears.

Torey Hayden in *One Child* recounts a horrific incident when Sheila is raped by an uncle. Though the little girl recovers from the physical wounds that nearly kill her she is unable to release the emotional pain; in fact Sheila is a child that never cries. "I don't never cry," she informed Torey. "Ain't nobody can hurt me that ways." A while after the rape Torey's boyfriend bought Sheila a dress to wear. Sheila is so surprised and moved that she begins to cry. Torey writes, "The time had finally come. The time I had been waiting for through all these long months that I knew sooner or later had to occur. Now it was here." At this point Torey gathers little Sheila into her arms and hugs her tightly. "She cried and cried, and cried. I simply held her and rocked the chair back and forth on its rear legs, feeling my arms and chest get damp from the tears and her hot breath and the smallness of the room."

On another occasion when the painful subject of separation comes up Torey just held the child and rocked her, knowing that words would not help. Nevertheless Torey questions the rightness of the relationship that had grown up between them. "Had I gotten too involved, I wondered? Despite her apparent progress, had I let her grow too dependent on me? Would it have been better to have left her as I found her in January and simply taught her, rather than accustomed her to the everyday trials of loving someone?" Despite this dilemma Torey goes ahead reading, talking to, loving, holding and rocking Sheila who eventually leaves the class a very different little girl from the one who entered it. Torey had taken a risk and broken all the professional rules of non-involvement but had succeeded where others had failed. Non-involvement may be possible when you see a client for half-an-hour once a month but it is impossible to maintain within the Christian family. The route then must be one of love within safe boundaries.

It is good to remember John, "the disciple whom Jesus loved," reclining next to Jesus at the last supper and actually "leaning back against Jesus" (John 13:23–25). We see that Jesus got involved in loving His disciples and allowed them to come emotionally and physically close to Him. He should be our example.

Having examined the potentially healing relationship between the counsellor and counsellee, we will continue by looking briefly at various approaches to counselling, enlarging on one particular approach.

8

THE APPROACH

A person seeks help from a counsellor because he is dissatisfied with his life or his way of coping with it. And he seems unable to effect change on his own.

There are three major steps in the therapeutic process, which are quite simply:

– commencing therapy
– being in therapy
– concluding therapy

These may seem rather obvious but in fact people can appear to be "in therapy", which is stage two when they have never actually passed through stage one. They therefore never make real headway.

One of the reasons we would not suggest to a person that he comes for counselling is because the responsibility for commencing belongs to the counsellee. Asking for help then is the first step to healing. Moving on to stage two may occur quickly or slowly and in some cases never. A person may come for help, feel safe enough, understand the boundaries and requirements, possess the energy to get down to work immediately and by the end of the first session "be in therapy".

I remember once a determined-looking lady asking for help. On the first visit she outlined the problem and gave me a potted history. I responded by setting up a series of appointments and suggested she do some homework in preparation. I asked her to keep a note book to bring to the next appointment. She was to note down anything that happened – that she thought or dreamed that could in any way be relevant to her problem.

The next session she came armed with her note book. Settling into the chair she began to tell me some relevant happenings of the previous week and her reactions and responses to them. She had made some connections with her childhood and in her prayer times had felt God was showing her some of the roots of her problem. She said she would like to start by working on these roots. She then asked if she could sit on the floor where she felt she would be freer to express anything that came up. This lady confronted her problems with determination and moved easily and quickly from stage one to stage two. Without any hesitation she was "in therapy".

In contrast a person may come for help and even after four sessions not really have begun. He is apparently not in the process of healing. He may be nervous and cannot relax sufficiently. He may not trust the counsellor and so spends the first four sessions testing him out before he can commit to work with him. He may still be hoping the counsellor will take responsibility for solving his problems and be waiting for solutions to be given him. He may even be expecting his problems to go away without paying the price of changing. All of this needs patience and understanding on the counsellor's part. After four sessions the counsellor should be able to discern if the counsellee is a non-starter or just a slow beginner.

Helpful reminder

After that first interview the counsellor has the difficult task of finding a way of helping a person through to a healthier way of living. It is good to bear in mind the following points about the counsellee.

He has a fallen nature
Not only the whole human race but every part of man has been affected by the fall. "Sin entered the world through

one man, and death through sin, and in this way death came to all men, because all sinned . . ." (Rom. 5:12).

This sin factor must be taken into account and recognised as part of the problem the counsellee is facing. Every counsellee will have his ongoing battle with wrong attitudes and sinful behaviour.

He is a complex human being

He is not just a spiritual being that needs to know God better. Nor is he just an emotional one that needs to express his feelings more freely. Neither is he just a physical body that may need a lot more exercise! Nor is he just a rational or social person who needs his thinking and behaviour changed. He is all of these things rolled into one. If one area malfunctions then every other area will be affected.

He is a unique person

There has never been anyone quite like him before or since! He has a unique past history – generationally, culturally and experientially. He is made up of the distant past – of the generations before him, and the immediate past – his own particular experience of life from conception on till the present. He has perceived and drawn conclusions about life that have produced a very intricate and complicated web of thinking, feeling and behaving. This way of being is his reality. It may not be the best or the most fulfilling way of being but it is all he is and knows. Any change will seem strange and frightening and even impossible.

He is more than he seems

Psychologists tell us that a person possesses three levels of consciousness. By a process of gating we suppress and repress unwanted material into the lower levels of the subconscious and unconscious. Though a counsellee may therefore relate his problems to a counsellor quite truthfully, the information stored in his conscious mind, which he chooses to communicate, is just part of the story; the tip of the iceberg. There is always a mine of material tucked away in his unconscious that will be exerting a strong influence upon his life.

God knows everything about him

However complex he is, however unique, however fallen, however much is hidden away within him, God knows him intimately.

> O LORD, you have searched me
> and you know me.
> You know when I sit and when I rise;
> you perceive my thoughts from afar.
> You discern my going out and my lying down;
> you are familiar with all my ways.
> Before a word is on my tongue you know it completely,
> 　O LORD.
>
> 　　　　　　　　　　　　　　　　[Ps.139:1–4]

As I pray for a counsellee I always remind myself that there is no way I can get past this "gating" process into the repressed material, but Jesus is able to do so by His Holy Spirit. There are no closed-off areas He cannot reach. "He who searches our hearts knows the mind of the Spirit, because the Spirit intercedes for the saints in accordance with God's will" (Rom. 8:27). God knows everything that has gone into making a man the person he is. He will also know the best way of helping him to deal with his problems.

With all this in mind the counsellor will now seek a way of assisting the counsellee to a healthier, happier and freer existence.

Psychotherapy has a Heinz 57 variety of approaches. Each has its own particular language and technique. Because of the absolute uniqueness of each individual no one approach would seem adequate. It is good if possible to be acquainted with some of the different schools of thought and thus be able to adapt and use what would seem appropriate in a given situation.

There are several very good and informative books that are helpful to read; I would especially recommend *Roots and Shoots* by Roger Hurding, a Christian psychologist. Meanwhile the following brief and simple pointers may be of help.

Some secular approaches

The Psychoanalytical approach
The focus here is on the material hidden in the depths of the unconscious. Free association, fantasies, and dream interpretation are all used to unlock this material and reinterpret it. The objective is to produce a greater integration and harmony within the client. We are indebted to Freud for much of the early thinking here.

The Cognitive approach
The basic assumption here is that the way a person thinks affects his emotions and his behaviour. Change a person's way of thinking and in turn his feelings and behaviour will change. In the secular world Albert Ellis's Rational Emotive Therapy is associated with this method.

A Christian counsellor who follows this approach has said, "All change in the quality of a person's life must grow out of a change in his or her vision of reality" (*Fully Human, Fully Alive*, John Powell). Another Christian counsellor writes, "The counselling method taught in this book brings talk therapy and cognitive behaviour change methods together. The counsellor attempts to help the counsellee discover his harmful cognitions, grasp their false character, and replace them with the truth." He goes on to say that, "This agreeable framework is currently known as cognitive psychology" (*Telling the Truth to Troubled Minds*, William Backus). Lawrence J Crabb, yet another well known Christian counsellor would also adhere to this method.

Transactional Analysis
Of all the modern therapies this has given us a popular and easily understood approach to people and their problems.

Eric Bern the founder of Transactional Analysis (TA) identifies three ego states: the Parent, the Adult and the Child. The "Parent" voice within a person may be either one of criticism and prejudice, full of "oughts, shoulds and don'ts", or one of nurture and encouragement. The "Child" is the voice of feelings, it is a set of attitudes and behaviour patterns formed in childhood. According to how the "Child" perceives the "Parent" voice it will be either an "Adapted Child", fearful and rejected or a "Free Child", secure and creative. The "Adult" is the monitoring voice, tuned into present reality. When in working order the "Adult" sifts the messages coming from both the "Parent" and the "Child" and will respond with the truth.

This approach is rational and analytical. It encourages responsibility for self and is therefore conducive to the growth of the individual. It lends itself to Christian adaptation. Jean Morrison has written two useful books called *A Tool for Christians* (*Books 1 & 2*), "to teach the use of Transactional Analysis to those who care about growth in loving relationships within the Christian community".

In terms of helping a counsellee understand his inner conflicts we have found this method very helpful. A counsellee can quickly identify an inner, critical parent voice condemning his inner child and causing feelings of rejection and fear. Frequently the critical voice is recognised as that once used by a past authority figure and now used by the counsellee to condemn himself. The counsellor can then encourage the adult part of the counsellee to look at the truth of the matter. "Is the 'child' so bad, so worthless, such a nuisance. How does God view that child?" Gradually, in the light of the truth, a counsellee can be encouraged to drop the critical parent voice and become more a nurturing parent to his own inner child.

The Feeling therapies

Janov's "Primal therapy", Perls' "Gestalt therapy" and Jackin's "Re-evaluation therapy" all fall into this category.

Janov believes that abreaction (or re-living past experiences with all the associated emotions) is a means of integrating a person. Re-evaluation therapy would also encourage expression of feelings associated with past hurt. Energy once needed to suppress pain would then be freed to cope properly with present day situations. Gestalt therapy is not so much an exploration of the past but an experience of the "here and now". It is, however, an experiential approach rather than a cognitive or interpretive one. Strong expression of emotion is encouraged and various techniques are used to induce this.

The Behaviourist approach

Those who work in this field seek to modify or to change a person's negative behaviour by desensitisation, by rewards and punishments, by modelling and demonstration. Healthier behaviour, it is hoped, will produce changes in thinking and feeling. B F Skinner is associated with this thesis.

Christian counselling will of necessity include some discussion, even advice, on behaviour. Help is often needed to change unbiblical behaviour to more Christ-like behaviour.

A layman could feel lost in such a maze of theories where all seem to make some sense and contain some truth. For the practice of Christian counselling it is preferable to hold a fairly eclectic approach. Some Christian counselling has simply reflected the secular trends. We may theoretically adhere to, or feel more comfortable with one theory or another, but our practice will contain elements from all.

Divergent philosophies

However in looking to secular psychology for understanding, a Christian could find himself subtly influenced by the philosophies behind the various approaches. The three main dangers seem to be the following.

Humanism

This is "a view of life that centres its focus on humanity, its potential and achievements" (*Roots and Shoots*, Roger Hurding). It sees man in a very optimistic light; perceiving him as basically good and naturally desiring to grow and change. It elevates man to a plane where God is irrelevant and unnecessary.

Reductionism

This is a tendency to dehumanise man, reducing him to the level of an animal that can be trained or a machine that runs by programming, instead of a complex being made in the image of God.

Transpersonalism

This philosophy seeks for meaning and fulfilment beyond the self. It is existential and mystical, embracing much Eastern thinking and religion. Influences come from zen buddhism and yoga, as well as other non-Christian mystical traditions. It encourages man to move beyond his conscious self and discover his transcendent self. Certain breathing and visualisation techniques are used to achieve this. Because of the meditative and spiritual nature of transpersonal psychology Christians are sometimes drawn towards it not realising the dangers. Our materialistic and rationalistic society has created a spiritual vacuum. This has caused many people to look for a spiritual experience in potentially harmful places. As Roger Hurding says: "The believer needs to sift the assumptions, aims and methods of transpersonalism in the light of God's revelation." Especially when the techniques used are ones that would open the user up to "unknown spiritual and psychic forces" (*Roots and Shoots*). Man's hunger is for God; to know Him and to be known by Him. The Christian Church needs to rediscover the riches of true meditation and spirituality based on the word of God, which through Christ, touches the heart of God.

The Eclectic approach

It is important therefore to keep in mind the biblical view of man, at the same time as recognising that the secular world can give us useful pointers as we attempt to help people overcome a variety of problems.

I find it interesting to look back through my diary and see that during the course of one week I used something from most of the above approaches. I spent time with a woman who had been molested sexually by a family friend when she was quite a small child. We encouraged her to express the feelings of fear and anger that she had been unable to express at the time. We took her through some inner-healing and she renounced the inner vows she had made as a child "never to trust a man". We ended by suggesting some activity that would help her deal with her mistrust of the opposite sex and move positively towards friendship with one or two men.

Another session was spent talking to a lady with marriage problems. We talked about more assertive behaviour. Another appointment was with a family. We worked together with the whole family on finding better ways of relating to one another. Towards the end of the week I saw two couples who were having sexual problems. One couple was obviously in need of some inner healing as well as ongoing counselling. The other couple just needed some practical advice. The rest of the time was taken up with long-term counsellees with whom I worked on change in every area of their lives.

With the last group we invited the Holy Spirit to bring to the surface what He wanted to deal with on that day. As the memories came up into the conscious mind some strong feelings were expressed in each case. This was followed by prayer for healing of those memories. Sometimes forgiveness needed to be released; sometimes inner vows had to be broken. With each we spent time talking through new insights that had come as God had surfaced more of that hidden pain from the past.

As we have already stated, an eclectic approach would seem to be necessary given the variety of people's problems and the uniqueness of each individual. However, we frequently find God moving in one particular direction with the counsellees that come to us. It is this direction that we will endeavour to describe.

One of the things we value is the working of the Holy Spirit. We do not lead the way. He leads and we follow, trying to trace His work in the person. The Son "does only what he sees the Father doing" (John 5:19 Living Bible). As we have been witnessing God at work in people's lives through the Spirit we have sought to track His activity. The following approach would seem to be in line with what God is doing. It also happens to coincide partially with some secular procedures which we will mention. These have never led us but only reinforced us and encouraged us to continue.

Though this approach seems to be one that works well, because we are committed to track God, we are continually open to change and to develop it in a different way. By sharing our experience we are not thereby committed to stay within the confines of any one method we outline.

9

THE CATHARTIC EXPERIENCE

A large middle-aged lady lay on the hard floor of a school gymnasium. The Holy Spirit had been invited to come and minister to a sizeable gathering of people and this particular lady had slumped to the ground. As she "rested in the Spirit" I knelt beside her and prayed that God would penetrate the inner recesses of her being with His healing power. As I did so she began to tremble a little. I continued to pray and the trembling increased until she seemed to be almost bouncing on the floor. At this point she started to moan and then cry. The crying gradually became like that of a small child who sounded terrified and desperate. I continued praying and asked God to release all the pain in that child's heart. She cried, screamed and rolled around in agony for about twenty minutes. Slowly the emotion subsided and she lay quietly. I suggested she forgave those who had hurt her so badly and she nodded in agreement. I sat in silence allowing her to make her own response to God. I sensed this was a sovereign work of God and that what He had begun He would finish. After a while she opened her eyes, looked at me and smiled. "Phew!" she said, "That was amazing! I was taken back to a time when I was about three and was put into an isolation hospital. It was so painful being taken away from my mother. I needed her so badly."

On another occasion we were at a meeting in a beautiful old cathedral church in the north of England. At the end of the service we offered to pray for anyone with a need, whether physical, emotional or spiritual. The people queued up in an orderly fashion. It had been a very quiet evening but the power of God was quite evidently at work. The team of people with us worked in twos, some at the communion rails, others in the choir stalls. Suddenly a commotion broke out at the rails. A young man (probably in his twenties) began to shake very violently. He seemed to be in considerable distress. His shaking became so strong the rails were in danger of being pulled from the ground. My husband went to the rescue and managed to lay the young man on the stone floor, where he continued to thrash around uncontrollably. With one knee on the man's chest David asked the Lord to free him and heal him. Gradually the manifestation died down. When he was eventually able to speak he seemed to be bewildered by what had happened and could not understand it. David asked him if he had ever felt like that before. "Only once," he replied. "About a year ago I had a car accident and I had a similar feeling." When asked what had happened to him then, he replied, "Nothing." He had walked away from the accident and was driving again the next day. Had he just experienced the "shock" which he had suppressed at the time of the accident? It seemed as though a canister of compressed energy had been released in him.

These two examples are taken from among hundreds of similar instances that our teams have witnessed over the past six years, while ministering all over the British Isles, parts of Europe, the United States, Israel, Africa, India, Australia, New Zealand, and the Far East. In every place visited we have seen similar manifestations. For some, like the woman I mentioned, it became clear what had been happening; for others, like the young man, we could only surmise. Little by little we have tried to come to an understanding. This is still growing and open to change as we continue witnessing the amazing power of God at work in people's lives. It is impossible to be definitive about our observations regarding the phenomenology of the Holy Spirit but certain things seem to occur consistently wherever we have been, and to have become a part of our normal expectation.

The work of the Holy Spirit in large meetings

Anointing

Time and again we have seen people being anointed with gifts of the Holy Spirit. They have spoken in tongues, and prophesied, as they did in the early Church (Acts 2:8). Many have experienced burning and tingling hands which seems to suggest an anointing for healing the sick in the power of the Holy Spirit.

Intercession and praise

At times, waves of intercession have moved over an entire gathering and at other times it has been impossible to stick to the programme as a spirit of joy and praise has flowed from the congregation.

Demonic activity

In the New Testament we read of demons crying out when Jesus was present (Luke 4:33,41). We have also witnessed the power of the Holy Spirit to disturb demons and then to deliver people from them, although it would be quite wrong to attribute all crying out to the presence of demons.

Healing

Most commonly we have seen the power of God coming to heal. One afternoon in a conference in Australia God came in power and healed a number of backs. There were many "Oohs" and "Aahs" as this happened. Very often the sickness is a spiritual one. Sin and guilt have robbed a person of their intimacy with God. Tears of repentance and thankfulness are shed as God's healing power sets them free. Many times people are born again of the Spirit of God. This has not been the result of anyone witnessing to them or a sermon being particularly evangelistic but because God's Spirit was at work manifestly in their presence.

Healing of the emotions
Frequently emotions are the target for God's healing power. For the purposes of this book we will look more closely at this particular work of the Holy Spirit.

The gating process

The concept of the three levels of consciousness, which we have already mentioned, was first developed by Freud. The conscious level is where we are aware of all that is happening here and now. The sub-conscious level is where we store material that is available for recall at any time. Then there is the unconscious level where we store all the memories, experiences and emotions that we cannot voluntarily recall. We function mostly on the first two levels and by a process of gating we block and repress any material passing from the lower levels into the upper ones. Though the content of our unconscious mind may not be able to be brought into conscious awareness, it can, nevertheless, still exert considerable influence upon us.

If these lower levels contain a lot of negative experiences then we may be struggling continually with bad or difficult feelings we cannot understand such as fear, anxiety, anger, panic, insecurity, tension and depression. These may be accompanied by unexplained physical symptoms.

Nothing is beyond God's reach. Jesus was able to pass through the closed doors of the upper room where the disciples were hiding after the crucifixion "with the doors locked for fear . . . Jesus came and stood among them" (John 20:19). Again we read "Though the doors were locked Jesus came and stood among them" (John 20:26). Our psychological "gating" poses no problems for Jesus! With the lady on the gymnasium floor, He entered into a deep level of her being and exploded a repressed experience. The Holy Spirit caused her to "abreact", or relive, the memory in an emotional way. She experienced a variety of strong feelings. Panic, longing, loneliness, anger and despair were all expressed during those minutes on the floor. The young man in the cathedral went through twenty minutes or so of terror. The only similar feeling he could recollect was a fleeting one following a car accident. From his own account he had obviously suppressed his feelings of shock and fear, pulled himself together and was driving the next day. The event seemed to have been pushed down into some corner of his subconscious. The accompanying feelings, however, seem to have been either totally aborted, or repressed to a deep level of the unconscious mind. These were unavailable to him until the Holy Spirit by-passed the gating process and surfaced those negative and potentially damaging feelings.

Aldous Huxley writes about the phenomena of sobbing, shaking and twitching resulting in a sense of liberation and openness to healing.

This is a phenomenon I have observed in others and experienced in myself, and seems to be one of the ways in which the deeper self rids itself of the impediments which the conscious superficial ego puts in its way. Sometimes there is a recall of buried material, with abreactions. But by no means always. And when there is no such recall, many of its beneficent results seem to be obtained when the deeper self sets up this disturbance in the organism – a disturbance which evidently loosens many of the visceral and muscular knots, which are the results and counterparts of psychological knots. Disturbances of this kind were common among the early Friends – and led to their being called Quakers. 'Quaking' is evidently a kind of somatic equivalent of confession and absolution, of recall of buried memories and abreaction to them, with dissipation of their power to go on doing harm. We should be grateful for the smallest and oddest

mercies – and this quaking is evidently one of them,
and by no means the smallest [Quoted in *Gestalt Is*,
J O Stevens.]

This comment is fascinating. What psychotherapists have
induced deliberately and sometimes accidentally, the Holy
Spirit has produced spontaneously.

The natural healing sequence

It would seem that good, positive experiences of life leave
us feeling fulfilled and satisfied. These experiences have a
rounded-off well finished feeling to them. Even unhappy
experiences properly handled seem to have a similar effect.
I remember a friend telling me about a close and fulfilling
relationship she had experienced with another woman who
had died of cancer. "When she died I didn't feel depleted, I
felt as if something had been added to me. I was left richer
not poorer." There had been nothing ragged or unfinished
about that experience.

Owing to our misconceptions about emotion many of our
experiences through life, from babyhood on, have had no
closure to them and have remained unhealed. We have
been left with unresolved relationships and problems,
unforgiven hurts and unexpressed pain, all stuffed down
inside ourselves, below the level of our consciousness. We
have never known how to handle these and have hoped
they would just disappear or dissolve in time.

The problem lies largely in our cultural attitude towards
feelings and our misunderstanding of catharsis and its
healing qualities.

John Powell's description of "fully alive" people includes the fact that "they are comfortable with and open to
the full experience and expression of all human emotions.
Such people are vibrantly alive in mind, heart and will." He
also states that "the full and free experience and expression
of all our feelings is necessary for personal peace and
meaningful relationships" (*Fully Human, Fully Alive*).

Many of the Bible characters seem to bear out this truth.
Jesus wept at the grave of Lazarus. We read that He was
"deeply moved in spirit and troubled" (John 11:33).
Joseph wept when his brothers came down from Canaan to
Egypt. "Deeply moved at the sight of his brother, Joseph
hurried out and looked for a place to weep. He went into
his private room and wept there" (Gen. 43:30). When he
eventually made himself known to his brothers we read
that "he wept so loudly that the Egyptians heard him and
Pharaoh's household heard about it." (Gen. 45:2). David
wept and mourned openly when Saul and Jonathan were
killed. "David and all the men with him took hold of their
clothes and tore them. They mourned and wept and fasted
till evening for Saul and his son Jonathan" (2 Sam. 1:11,
12). When Peter denied Jesus and the cock crowed the
second time "he broke down and wept" (Mark 14:72). We
could go on to mention many other such instances of
expression of feeling in the Bible.

When God created man He put within him the ability to
heal himself. For example when he cuts his finger a whole
process is set in motion which continues until the new skin
has formed over the wound. The healing is complete
leaving only a scar. With the coming of Jesus the healing of
man's spiritual sickness and alienation through sin was
made possible. But God is concerned with the whole of
man – his physical, spiritual, mental, social and emotional
well-being. He has also put within him the ability to recover
from emotional hurt and distress.

Unfortunately this very process of recovery has become
turned around into something many people are ashamed
of. Today "repression is so much a way of life that many of
us view being 'emotional' and showing feelings as 'acting
neurotic'. We come to believe that self-control is the
hallmark of health and any show of feeling is tarred with the
brush of hysteria. The fact that feelings are such a threat to
us indicates how much pain we have to defend against"
(*Prisoners of Pain*, Arthur Janov).

The proper, natural healing process is thought to be

neurotic. What is natural and healthy is said to be unnatural, irrational, uncontrolled, unhealthy and weak. Most of us have lost the ability to let the normal healing processes operate in the way they were created to do – by feeling, reacting to and discharging the pain of the hurt.

It is the most natural thing to react to pain. If one is cut or burned, for example, one cries or screams, and jumps around shaking the injured part. Such natural responses help consume the energy of the pain and eventually dispel it. But when pain is excessive and is repressed, energy is not consumed. It remains within as a constant inner force. The healing sequence is not run off and the wound not closed. For wounds to heal they have to hurt. The pain is part of the healing process.

In our present-day culture we abort this healing sequence again and again throughout our lifetime. This is the real neurotic behaviour – the "little boys don't cry" and "the stiff upper lip" syndrome. Our behaviour has been learned from our parents who in turn learned it from theirs. We have it taught by word and by example, until we too become adept at aborting the natural God-given healing sequence of feeling – expression.

"When feelings are suppressed they are mislabelled, denied and masked only to reappear as illness, fatigue, deadness or argumentativeness," (*Emotional Expression in Psychotherapy*, Pierce, Nichols and DuBrin).

The correct way to help children become emotionally healthy is to allow them their feelings and teach them how to discharge them in an appropriate way. Instead of popping the sticky sweet in a hurt child's mouth and laying down the foundation for "comfort eating" later on, a child should be allowed to discharge all the feelings of pain by crying, shaking, sobbing and talking, until the hurt is resolved and a normal equilibrium restored.

John Cleese explains how "the person on the healthy track has been getting rid of the various sadnesses that have come from all his many small losses by feeling them at the time. To take a silly example, if it takes 1,000 sadness units to separate from Mum, the healthy-track child has been able to do them one at a time. So each loss is small and manageable. But the person on the unhealthy track has got all those units piled up there behind the barrier" (*Families and How to Survive Them*, John Cleese and Robin Skynner).

Most of us were not shown how to be emotionally healthy. We live with anxiety, tension, depression, high blood pressure, raised pulse rate, back ache, indigestion, tightness in the chest, headache, palpitations and many such psychosomatic symptoms. We are sick and in need of God's healing.

Completing the aborted sequence

God made us and knows us intimately, "For you created my inmost being; you knit me together in my mother's womb," (Ps. 139:13). Our conscious, sub-conscious and unconscious are all available to Him. He knows the secrets of our hearts and knows how best to heal us. Again and again we have watched God move sovereignly upon men and women causing them to abreact (relive) a past painful experience with all the accompanying feelings being energetically expressed. In so doing He brings completion to an aborted process. The lady on the gymnasium floor needed to express all the painful feelings of separation from her mother at a time when she was too young to bear it. The natural healing sequence of feeling expression had most probably been impossible at the time but under the power of God it was recalled and the interrupted sequence was completed.

Catharsis as part of healing

"Catharsis in psychoanalysis describes the purifying, purging, relaxing, releasing effect of a dramatic emotional reliving of experiences from the past, particularly so if, at that time the strong emotions aroused were only partially expressed, suppressed or entirely repressed" (*Clinical Theology*, Frank Lake).

Or as it has been elsewhere described, "Catharsis is the completion of an interrupted emotional action sequence," (*Emotional Expression in Psychotherapy*, Pierce, Nichols and DuBrin).

As we will see later catharsis or feeling expression on its own is not usually enough. It will bring healing providing it conveys insight and leads to new thinking and changed behaviour.

Catharsis helps people re-evaluate their early painful experiences and view them in a more accurate light. It also helps people to change their patterns of emotional repression. If one avoids facing the reality of painful events from the past one can never release them. Without becoming more feelingful, one cannot enter fully into life in the present.

As we have already emphasised each of us is wonderfully unique. The presenting, or manifest, problem for one person may sound similar to that of another. But the fact is not only is it owned by a totally different person, but its roots will be in a different soil and its development yet again in a different environment. Therefore to suggest that one approach is right for every troubled person would be to ignore this uniqueness. We must pray that God will guide us to the most effective ministry for each counsellee. However, watching God sovereignly at work in the way we have described, we have seen catharsis as part of the healing process in hundreds of different lives.

Our experience of this began in these larger gatherings where God effected the expression of feelings. It was in no way suggested or manipulated and the only possible explanation of what happened seems to have been God Himself. I often watch what is happening with awe and think to myself, "That can only be God." Our creator knows what He is doing and how best to heal us of the wounds and hurts that we have received. Having witnessed this so often we can only say that we believe that catharsis is often the vital key in the healing process. The question is: How can we incorporate it into the counselling situation?

By way of an answer we turn our attention now away from the large meeting to the intimacy of the counselling room, where we will examine catharsis and its effects in more detail.

10

CATHARSIS IN COUNSELLING

A number of things should occur during the first interview with a new counsellee. There should be the following components.

A realistic sharing by the counsellee

The counsellor needs of course to be aware of the fact that the counsellee will probably not have sufficient insight or confidence at this stage to be able to share fully, but he should aim to share the present problem and his past history.

An assessment and tentative diagnosis by the counsellor

This should determine whether the counsellee needs referral to a professional counsellor or whether the sort of help available in the local church would be sufficient. It may not always be possible to make a diagnosis at such an early stage. A counsellee may not always be truthful about the severity of the problem. One such counsellee only told her counsellor at the end of the fourth interview that she had several times attempted suicide and as a result had been admitted to a psychiatric hospital for a short stay.

The first interview should also enable the counsellor to decide on the type of counselling needed and the right sort of counsellor for that particular person. For example I once saw a lady who by my assessment needed more directive counselling than I would give her. Her life was quite chaotic and she seemed to have little idea of how to run her home or to organise her time. She had received very poor modelling from her mother and her greatest need at that time was for someone to come alongside and help her sort through her priorities and help her to bring some order to her chaos. I therefore suggested one or two names of people I felt would be able to help her. I agreed to approach one of these on her behalf. Subsequent sessions were conducted by the new counsellor.

By the end of the first interview a fairly clear picture should have emerged covering the background and present difficulties and an assessment of the inner strength of the counsellee. Would the person be able to cope with the hard work involved in becoming whole? Be able to weather the pain and conflict on the road to wholeness? Be able to sustain a relationship with the counsellor that would be therapeutic? And can you, the counsellor, envisage a relationship developing between you or would you feel someone else to be more suitable?

If the counsellor decides to work with the counsellee they should finally make:

A *working agreement or contract*

This will include arrangements for the time and place. Also the boundaries should be discussed and agreed upon. The method of counselling should be made clear and the counsellee's responsibilities stated.

Encourage the counsellee to state his goals for counselling

The following mock-up of a first interview, put together from a mixture of interviews to protect individual identity, may help to clarify the procedures.

> Joy arrives for her first appointment. She appears nervous and is twisting her car keys round and round in her hand. She takes up a position on the edge of the chair opposite her counsellor.

Counsellor Joy, I'm glad you have come. It must have taken a lot of courage to do so. I need to make several things clear from the beginning. In this room you are quite safe. No one can hear you and we shall not be disturbed. Within these four walls you may say whatever you like and you may express whatever feelings you need to. Without your permission nothing will go beyond this place. So why not start by explaining why you have come to see me.

Joy [Very nervous and speaking in a jerky way.] Now that I'm here it all sounds so stupid! I'm afraid I am wasting your time. It's all so silly . . . [trails off].

Counsellor It's OK. We all have things that we find difficult to cope with at times. Try and tell me what has been troubling you.

Joy [Still twisting the keys frantically.] Well it's to do with our homegroup, at least not really. It's really to do with people. I'm so nervous with people. You could say I'm people phobic – it's so silly. I feel so anxious when I'm with lots of people. It's as if I'm going to choke.

With encouragement Joy tells the counsellor that she has always had a tendency to be nervous with people but that since she had a bad bout of 'flu last winter the nervousness has increased. She was beginning to make excuses in order to avoid social contact. She is employed as a secretary, unmarried and has no boyfriend. She is the youngest child of three. Her parents are still alive. Both were strict disciplinarians. She is not close to her family though she visits regularly. There have been no bad illnesses and no history of mental illness in the family.

While Joy talked about her childhood and her relationship with her parents, her eyes darted around the room and she twisted the keys more frantically than ever.

Counsellor   Well Joy, I think we should try and tackle the problem. It would seem to have some roots in the past and your relationship with your parents. Let's take our time and allow God to do the healing in His own way. Perhaps we should arrange four appointments to start with. How does that sound to you?

Counsellor's assessment: Joy has plenty of inner strength. She is not a passive, dependent type of person and should be able to take responsibility and be capable of hard work. However, she is excessively nervous and tense and is using a lot of energy to keep the feelings under control. At some stage she will most likely fall apart, probably sooner rather than later. I shall need the support of another counsellor and Joy will need back-up support from friends if we are to cope with the next few weeks.

Counsellor   Joy, have you got some support besides
                 your homegroup: someone you know well
                 who you can really rely upon being there if
                 you need extra help outside the counselling
                 sessions?

Joy   Yes, I share a flat with a friend. She is older
                 and very sensible. I can tell her most things.
                 She knows I am here tonight.

Counsellor   Good. Now let's talk a bit about the
                 counselling procedure and before we part
                 we should set some goals for these times
                 together. But first I need to ask you if you
                 have any objection to my asking Ann Smith
                 to work with me? We always try and see
                 people in pairs, but the other person needs
                 to be someone you can relate to.

[They talked about the length of the sessions and Joy was
asked not to receive counselling elsewhere for the
duration of our ministry to her. They went on to discuss
the work involved in becoming whole.]

Counsellor   We shall be asking God to take you back to
                 the roots of the problem. You have prob-
                 ably never allowed yourself to feel the pain
                 and hurt of your childhood traumas and
                 memories. You were probably afraid you
                 would be punished if you made a fuss then.
                 But up here, in this room, that little girl has
                 permission to cry her tears, feel her pain
                 and open up the wounds for God to heal.
                 Your responsibility is to go with what is
                 happening inside you through the Holy
                 Spirit. Whatever God puts His finger on,
                 you need to bring out into the open and to
                 express the feelings about the memory.

Allow yourself to feel the experience. As you do so you will gain understanding and insight and God will begin to heal the hurts. Now before we pray and finish for today let's set some goals for our time together.

Joy   [Thinks for a while.] Well, I'd like to become a more relaxed person – not so nervous. And I would like to be able to enjoy a social occasion and not to feel as if I am going to choke to death every time I'm in a crowded room.

Counsellor   That sounds good.

They prayed and committed their future sessions to God. The first interview had taken an hour and a half but during that time a good amount of ground had been covered.

In subsequent appointments some things will need to be repeated. The procedures should be explained again. The need to express feelings will have to be restated. Permission to express every type of feeling that a memory evokes should be given – especially the feelings most abhorrent to the counsellee; ones that would have been most disapproved of in his childhood and therefore aborted by the counsellee.

It is important for a counsellee to realise that he is there to work and he should feel free to do that in whatever way suits him. Passivity should be discouraged. During subsequent sessions the time together will start with some talking about progress and any changes, insights or problems that have been experienced since the previous appointment.

The actual ministry time will then start with prayer; asking God to take control and to come by the power of His Holy Spirit to penetrate the inner recesses of the counsellee's being. It is important to wait and allow God plenty of time to begin His work. After a while we would ask the counsellee what was happening.

The following interview describes a fairly typical ministry time with a person who is committed to openness and has already stepped over the bridge to full expression of feeling.

Counsellor [After inviting the Holy Spirit to come and waiting for a while.] Ruth, what is happening?

Ruth I feel such a tightness in my chest, it really hurts me. [She clutches her chest and starts to moan.] It might stop hurting if I could make a noise.

Counsellor That's OK, make all the noise you want.

Ruth [Begins to groan, softly at first but gradually the volume increases and between the groans come words.] Oh, I feel so lonely, I'm all alone – there is no one there for me. There are so many people but no one there for me. I feel so frightened. [She begins to breathe faster and the groans turn into sobs. She is beginning to shake. The sobbing and shaking continue for several minutes.]

During this time the counsellors are praying quietly under their breath and now and again encourage Ruth to 'go with the feeling'. Eventually the crying decreases and the counsellee comes back to present reality.

Ruth Phew. That was a bad experience! It must have been my first day at nursery school. I felt so alone. No one seemed to be there for me. [Starts to cry again.] Don't leave me, please don't leave me. [Again she starts to abreact but this time with even more desperation. She clutches the counsellor's hand and shouts loudly.] Don't leave me alone. Please, please don't go. [The crying and sobbing continue for some time and then gradually begin to subside.]

Counsellor   How about forgiving Mummy for leaving you alone, and the teachers for not comforting you? Do you think you could do that?

Counsellee nods and begins to release forgiveness.

Counsellor   Now I'm going to pray and ask Jesus to come and heal that lonely, frightened little girl.

Having prayed there is a silent waiting for Jesus to do His work in Ruth's heart. After a while Ruth stirs, sits up and smiles.

Ruth   I think Jesus really loves that little girl. I've always rather despised her but I believe He accepts her. I felt just now that He really understood how she was feeling. It's funny but I've always been afraid of new places and strange faces. I think that nursery school experience had a lot to do with it. Also the fact that Mum and Dad didn't show their feelings and didn't like me to either. I was never able to tell them how much I hated that school.

It would be misleading to suggest that after such a short cathartic experience Ruth was now healed, though it was certainly an encouraging step forward. However, she may ventilate in a similar way over and over again before any real change in present-day feelings and attitudes is noticed. During the course of further ministry several inner vows she made as a child may come to light and have to be renounced and broken in Christ's name. New behaviour may have to be tried out and the bad feelings this produces worked through. Ways of feeling, thinking and behaving that have existed for some thirty years or more take time to change.

Not every counsellee is able to make such an easy connection with a childhood memory and express the feelings surrounding that memory so vigorously as in our example. Though a clear agreement has been made to express all the feelings that occur during ministry, many counsellees find it very hard to do so. Most people find it easier to talk about feelings than actually to feel them and release them. A counsellee may be able to describe a feeling quite fully. He may say, "I feel very sad – it's a lonely sad feeling – as if no one is there for me." This may be spoken in a sad, depressed voice but without any release of the feelings. Without this release the healing may only be superficial. It is as though the healing is of some faint memory in the past which remains detached from present reality until connected by real feelings. In contrast where the counsellee allows himself to get into the feelings and express them vigorously he will find himself reliving the past as if it were in the present – he is feeling it now. The experience unfolds and instead of repressing the feelings a second time they are fully felt and fully expressed. Instead of neurotic repression the counsellee experiences healthy expression. As this happens over and over his neurosis begins to lose its hold. His unhealthy way of being begins to change. Healthier and more fruitful ways of being are discovered.

Ways of helping

How may a counsellee be helped to express difficult feelings more fully?

1. By understanding the procedures and what is expected of him

This may need to be explained over and over again.

2. By making a contract

The counsellee should agree to try and express the feelings that surface. He needs to understand that it may be hard to take down his defences and push through the natural resistances but that he is responsible for doing this. He may need to give himself permission to express his feelings. This is especially necessary when past authority figures have disapproved of any expression of strong emotions.

3. By experimenting with different ways of working

The counsellor must give permission for a counsellee to try out new ways of working. One young woman had been coming for several weeks and only managing a very partial expression of feelings. After a few sessions we discussed the difficulty she had in fully releasing her feelings. "Perhaps I could try lying on the mattress," she said. "It might open me up if I were lying down. I would feel more vulnerable that way." She knew she had permission to experiment but had been reticent to do so. Our session that day was in fact much more productive. Her experiment worked!

4. By empathy

As the counsellee describes the picture, memory or feeling coming up, the counsellor responds with empathy. "It sounds as if you were very lonely and sad at that time. Stay with that feeling of sadness! Tell me how that little girl is feeling?"

Empathy will often encourage a counsellee to keep going and stay with the pain until it is fully expressed instead of being suppressed once more.

5. By encouraging

This may mean giving permission again and again. "It's OK to feel those feelings – I know it's hard to go with the pain, but you are doing well. You don't have to push them down, just let them come up and express them." And when the counsellee begins to do this keep encouraging. "That's good! You're doing well! Keep going."

6. By role-play

If the counsellee has described a particular memory the counsellor may suggest that he goes back into the memory and talks to the people concerned. "Go back to the kitchen. Talk to Mummy. Tell her how you feel." As the counsellee begins to role-play the feelings may come up with considerable force.

One young counsellee described a dream in which she had seen a certain man coming towards her. This had caused such panic that she had woken from her sleep. She was encouraged to go back into it and talk to the man in her dream. As she began to speak to him her feelings erupted and she was spun back in time to a terrible experience of being sexually attacked by a strange man. She began to scream in panic. She continued to relive this painful childhood experience for about ten minutes, expressing all the feelings she had suppressed at the time.

7. By blocking a particular defence mechanism

Some counsellees will start to rock or swallow hard as the pain mounts and they automatically start pushing it down. Others will go very still and silent as if they were disappearing inside themselves. Yet others will draw away from any physical contact and refuse any support. Some will even black out as the pain becomes acute. As already mentioned when illustrating another point, a woman I worked with for some time would always hyperventilate when fearful memories started to surface. The only way of countering this was to teach her to cry or scream. In other words to expel breath rather than to draw it in.

Defence mechanisms are best dealt with patiently and kindly. They need to be pointed out clearly but should not be torn down thoughtlessly. The counsellor and counsellee need to work together to dismantle such defences.

I remember working with a counsellee who always drew further and further away from me as the session progressed. On one occasion, after pointing this out, I said I was going to put my hand on her shoulder and that she should try and stick with the feelings that came up as a result. It was painful for her to have to face the extreme "touch-starvation" she had endured as a child. To avoid touch of any kind was to avoid facing the pain and the yearning that she had for it.

8. By touching

Touching a counsellee may give him the support needed to explore a painful area of his life. In ministry it is good to sit alongside a counsellee holding his hand lightly or laying one's hand gently on his arm. A gentle touch is just sufficient for him to know someone is there and ready to give him support and help whenever it is needed. Tenderness conveyed in a touch may also provide the trigger needed to surface the blocked feelings.

9. By working with present feelings

One of the most successful ways of encouraging catharsis is to work with the present feelings of a counsellee which may be caused by a recent experience or relationship problem. For this to be possible, part of the contract, as we have seen already, must include truth and openness with one another.

I learned the value of this openness very early on during some ministry I received from a married couple. After one session I felt that the man had been a little off-hand with me and thinking about it afterwards I decided that he was probably bored with his part in ministering to me. I didn't feel particularly bad about this, but keen to let him off the hook, I found an opportunity to talk to his wife and suggested that he be free not to come to the next session. "I know he is busy," I said, "and he must be awfully bored with me twittering on." She looked at me in amazement. "What are you talking about?" she asked. "He's not bored at all; he's really keen to go on with the ministry. Perhaps you are putting some feelings on to him that don't belong to him." This gave me something to think about but didn't alter the way I felt.

The next session came around and the subject came up again. I began to describe how I felt about it. In the middle of the conversation the husband had to leave the room for some reason. As he went out of the door my feelings surfaced and I completely fell apart. By the time he came back into the room I was expressing and ventilating a lot of anger and hurt over my own father being too busy and too tired to give me much attention. This incident provided me with an experience of transference at first hand. It made me realise how easily it could become a stumbling block to healing, but with open admission of present feelings it had in fact become a stepping stone. More importantly, the ministry which followed that afternoon was possibly one of the most healing experiences I have ever had.

Catharsis has many beneficent results and has proved to be an important part of the healing process in many cases. We will go on to look at some of these results.

11

THE RESULTS OF CATHARSIS

People feel, think and act. Most people who seek help are usually preoccupied with their bad feelings or neurotic behaviour patterns. Few realise their thinking could also be faulty. Feeling, thinking and acting are so interdependent it is often difficult to disentangle them. A person may present the problem as one of behaviour but there are always thoughts and feelings behind that behaviour. Or the presenting problem may be a bad feeling, perhaps one of anxiety. Very soon however, the faulty thinking about life and whatever type of avoidance behaviour being practised will come to light.

A young girl came to see me feeling depressed and unhappy. "I feel so miserable, I wish I were dead," she said. Within a few minutes she had told me several times what a failure she thought she was and that God couldn't approve of her. She said she thought others despised and condemned her for being a failure. The result of the bad feelings and the wrong thinking was social withdrawal. Her problem couldn't be treated just as one of feelings or behaviour or even thinking. Therefore if any help is to be beneficial it has to be directed to all three areas.

Once a person can express his feelings fully in a counselling session, insight will nearly always follow. Present feelings, when expressed, act like a fuse trailing back to the real problem area. The connection is made emotionally and cognitively. Catharsis not only brings insight but releases energy. This energy, that was previously needed to suppress feelings, will now be available for forming new behaviour patterns.

In his book *The Different Drum*, Dr Scott Peck describes an experience of catharsis which changes his life. He is attending a twelve day "sensitivity group" as part of exploring a potential contract between the National Training Laboratories and the Army, in which he is employed. On the tenth day Scott Peck becomes very depressed and explains this to the T-group. The leader of the group suggests that "Scotty" should try and release some of the anger that the depression may be covering. As he does this he begins to get in touch with a tremendous feeling of tiredness. He writes, "Waves of fatigue begin to sweep over me. I started to sob." He continues to sob for half an hour. His true feelings of frustration with his job, his marriage, his years of training are surfacing. Dr Peck had not cried for thirty years; in fact not since he was a small boy. As a result of this experience he left the army and set up in private practice. In addition, he found that from that day on he was able to cry and even sob whenever appropriate. That one event changed his whole life. The catharsis led to clarification of what was causing the feelings of depression and this insight led to a change in his lifestyle.

The beneficent results of catharsis

It brings healing to hurt

Expression of feelings frequently releases into consciousness a past painful experience which had been pushed down into the unconscious. This causes an abreaction or reliving of the experience, but now with an expression of the once repressed feelings and an opportunity for real closure to the wound. Jesus, the one who suffered most terrible pain at the hands of man, is there by His Spirit to bring His healing to the smarting wound. And alongside are helpers who can add their love and support to His and be with the sufferer throughout his painful ordeal.

I like the way Frank Lake speaks about this experience of abreaction and the possible transformation of the past by reliving it in the presence of Christ and others. "The suffering is the same, and more may follow, but the meaning of it, how it is perceived, is transformed by the new metaphor: 'He is with me; they are with me; I am not alone.' So much of the horror of primal affliction lies in the solitariness of the suffering. With someone else there, in whose face I can see every familiar agony of my own soul, the intensity and bearableness of the suffering are quite changed" (*Tight Corners in Pastoral Counselling*).

Once a counsellee begins to express his feelings the dam will soon burst and years of suppressed pain will pour out. It is not unusual in counselling to see a person double up with pain or rock like a child in anguish. It is not wise to try and cut this process short. Sometimes the same feelings are expressed again and again. When it is finished there will be no more tears. Once the pain has been fully felt the healing will follow.

"In order for any wound to heal it has to hurt. The hurt is the healing process at work" (*Prisoners of Pain*, Arthur Janov).

It releases stress

Many people have not been able to cry since childhood and need that cathartic release of tears. Tears are an important element in emotional healing. I noticed an interesting snippet headed "Tearful Chemistry" published in the press recently:

There may appear to be little difference between tears caused by unhappiness or onions – but there is a marked chemical difference.

Scientists reporting at the First World Congress on Tears (held, believe it or not, in Dallas, Texas) have discovered that tears shed through emotion contain not only water and fatty substances but an enkaphalin, a naturally occurring, morphine-like substance which is known to play an important part in controlling emotions and pain. [Olivia Tims and Lorraine Fraser quoted in *The Times* 18.7.86.]

Arthur Janov writes of the high concentration of stress hormones found in tears. "Clearly, if there is indeed a release of stress hormones with tears, then the blocking of that release may result in the buildup of stress hormones. We believe that crying is an important biologic function and that the shedding of tears is central, not incidental, to the resolution of neurosis. There is no such thing as a 'talking cure'. The fact of weeping itself helps relieve suffering. Tears not only remove toxic substances of the eye, they also have a precise role in the removal of toxic biochemical substances from the entire system" (*Prisoners of Pain*).

Our bodies pay the price for the suppression of difficult feelings. When stress levels rise it wreaks havoc with our blood pressure, stomach juices and nervous system. A good cry could be all the medicine needed to prevent some of these stress-related diseases.

It brings insight
Often we are troubled by difficult feelings and try as we may we cannot make sense of them. These feelings may sometimes be causing wrong behaviour. Perhaps it even appears to be the other way around – a person's behaviour is apparently producing bad feelings.

A few years ago I was under a good deal of pressure with too big a counselling load. Those I looked to for advice told me I was doing too much and must cut back. Instead of taking proper notice of this I actually added two more people to my list that week! I knew something was wrong. I felt pressurised and tense but could not understand what was happening. The following week there was a special meeting in the church at the end of which the Holy Spirit came down on many people in power. I felt His presence on me and asked Him to do something to help me deal with the tension I was under. Quite quickly I felt pressure on my chest but was unable to express this in any way. The pressure increased and I became desperate for relief. I struggled for quite some time until I looked up and saw a young girl I knew well coming towards me. As she drew near I began to cry and all she had to do was to hold me as the tears flowed. The sobs increased in intensity and at the same time words were pouring out of me. At first they were just expressions of the present pressure, but gradually this changed and I felt the truth that had been eluding me all the week start to well up within me. "They mustn't be allowed to need with no one there . . . It's not right to have no one there when you need help." On and on I went in the same vein. As I spoke out the truth I began to see a picture in my mind of a huge pool of tears. The sadness of it nearly overwhelmed me. I drew closer to peer into it and to my horror saw my own reflection there and knew in that instant what had been happening. Releasing the feelings had led me to the inner truth behind the feelings and the reason for my behaviour became clear. I was projecting my own feelings of sadness and need on to everyone who asked for help. It wasn't their desperation I was feeling but my own past desperation for someone to be there when I needed them. The effect of that evening was twofold. First I felt a relief from the tension and stress I had been under and secondly I understood the reason I found it so difficult to say "No" in some situations. With some work on my part I knew it would be possible to change my behaviour.

There is no doubt that catharsis releases insight and understanding. As this gushes out with the feelings there is a sense of rightness and clarity about what is being expressed. "This is it; now I know." All the other very rational and logical explanations a counsellee may have verbally discussed with his counsellor fade into insignificance beside that clear, undeniable and often simple insight.

After a particularly productive outburst of feeling one woman told me with amazement, "I could never have understood that by just talking. I could have talked and talked for ever and never found the truth. It was only as I began to cry and those bad feelings came up that I realised I have lived in dread of my parents' anger all my life."

It is easier to search for answers to our problems rationally. The cognitive level feels safer than the emotional level for most people. We argue that the key to change is in understanding. In part it is but so often our understanding is partial, even faulty, and we can come up with an apparently logical answer which appears reasonable though in fact is far from the right one. Our emotional level leads more accurately to the truth. "This level (the affective) is probably the most powerful in a person's life. When we surface our feelings we get closer to our true selves. Feelings are the closest things that make up the real me" (*Friend to Friend*, David Stone and Larry Keefauver).

It facilitates the "putting off" and "putting on" process

Paul reminds the Ephesians that they were taught "to put off your old self, which is being corrupted by its deceitful desires; to be made new in the attitude of your minds; and to put on the new self, created to be like God in true righteousness and holiness" (Eph. 4:22, 23).

"Therefore, if anyone is in Christ, he is a new creation; the old has gone, the new has come!" (2 Cor. 5:17).

Change is an essential part of the gospel call to repentance. Yet often the change is blocked and Christians become disillusioned and discouraged by difficult feelings, wrong thoughts and bad habits. Change is never easy and often we battle with stubborn resistances within ourselves.

"Resistance to change is primarily a fear of relinquishing well tried defences against deeply repressed emotional pain" (*Clinical Theology*, Frank Lake). Our neurotic behaviour and reactions are ways of defending ourselves against feeling pain. We either adopt behaviour that takes the edge off our pain or behaviour that prevents it being stimulated. For instance a person brought up in an emotionally cold environment with no cuddles may be continually demanding love from others even using sex as a way of taking the edge off the pain of the unmet need for love and tenderness. Or conversely he may protect his pain by holding others at arm's length and by being distant and refusing to show or give affection. In both cases the unacceptable behaviour is an avoidance of pain. The way to change is through feeling the reality of that unmet need.

"One of the universal characteristics of neurotic people is their inability to change in spite of themselves. Neurosis is essentially stagnant-making behaviour consistent in its miserable predictability . . . allowing feeling back into our lives by experiencing the obstructed and obstructing pains of our early history brings back the ability to change, to move and, most importantly, to grow" (*Prisoners of Pain*, Arthur Janov).

a) Putting off. The first step in putting off present-day unproductive, unhealthy and often sinful behaviour patterns is, therefore, to return to the original trauma or traumas that set the behaviour in motion in the first place.

"Paradoxically the first step in letting go of the past involves returning to it cognitively and emotionally." (*Emotional Expression in Psychotherapy*, Pierce, Nichols and DuBrin).

Cognitively. The consequences of reliving childhood traumas is clarification of the way in which a person perceived these experiences. Understanding of the choices and vows that were unconsciously made at that time gives a person back the control of his life and freedom to remake the choices and renounce the vows.

Emotionally. When a person returns to a past scene emotionally it enables him somehow to tie up the loose ends. Many of these childhood traumas have had no fitting ending to them. By returning to them they can be appropriately finished. Feeling the pain and forgiving those who caused it brings closure and the past can be laid to rest. Once it is properly finished it ceases to have power to affect the present.

It is not always easy on the first occasion of ministry to forgive those who have hurt us. A Christian desiring God's will usually makes a rational choice to do so though the feelings may not at first accompany this decision. Expressing the pain that surrounds the hurt facilitates forgiving "from the heart". Sometimes it is necessary for a counsellee to release forgiveness repeatedly until eventually it is finally done. The counsellee will then express the satisfaction of having "finished something".

The need to mourn our losses fully is discussed by John Cleese and Robin Skynner.

Robin Because we've mourned whatever we've lost, we can let go of it and move on.

John But if you don't mourn it fully, you can't let go of it.

Robin That's right. The feeling of loss will hang around indefinitely, and you won't feel free to move on.

John So mourning – really feeling the pain of the loss – is not just natural, it actually accomplishes something.

[*Families and How to Survive Them.*]

b) Putting on. Part of the problem is the fact that suppression requires energy. The healing of inner pain will result in this energy becoming available to try out new behaviour.

Unhealed hurt can cause a bondage of the will and until it is healed a person will not experience the freedom to act in a more healthy manner. Once a counsellee has begun to deal effectively with his past, time should be spent in discussing new beliefs, choices and behaviour. The goals should be set and then milestones for achieving the goals laid down. For example one woman said her goal was to become a more affectionate and feeling person. We began with the practice of touch. During the next week she had consciously to try and take the initiative by touching her friends warmly on the arm or hand when talking to them.

Difficulties in "putting off" and "putting on"

Adopting new ways of thinking and behaving is the hardest step for a counsellee. The old ways are predictable, safe and habitual. When a person begins to try out new behaviour it seems at first as if he has stepped into an emotional minefield.

The three most common difficulties standing in the way of change are the binding power of fear, the strength of old habits and the lack of good motivation for change.

Fear of change

Even the contemplation of change can create fear. Painful and difficult a person's life may be but at least he is accustomed to it. It is familiar and predictable and there is security in knowing what to expect. John Powell sees fear of chaos as the root problem facing a person trying to change his vision of life. "There is a lingering fear that in giving up the old vision, which has provided predictability and consistency, I might fall into the chaos" (*Fully Human, Fully Alive*).

If the mere prospect of change is alarming the effecting of it is even more so. Frequently a counsellee will confide that the new behaviour "feels sinful" or "abnormal".

A woman who had been proudly self-sufficient all her life came to us for counselling. She had been very depressed for some time but had felt unable to ask for help. "What's the point of needing others; they are never there when you want them," she proclaimed, revealing her irrational belief. She wanted to be healed but whenever we held her hand and suggested she receive our support she became rigid with fear. She believed in "bearing one another's burdens" and was good at supporting others in trouble. But because of her own past deprivation and the irrational belief she consequently held she found the receiving of support herself both abnormal and frightening.

Strength of old habits
Change in some areas may be incredibly difficult. If we have acted in a certain way for any length of time it requires real determination to act in another way. Some time ago we moved a wardrobe from just outside our bedroom door. Though the space is visible for all to see and I have been passing it several times a day for weeks, I still find myself avoiding the space where the wardrobe used to be. Old habits die hard!

No good motive for change
Without good motivation positive change will be imposs- ible. In fact the motivation within the counsellee may even be one that will counter change.

Motives that counter change

These include the following desires:

- – to be supported by others
- – to have a comfortable and painless life
- – to have retribution
- – to make others change

Good motivation

When a counsellee finds difficulty in "putting off" the old and "putting on" the new, only a good motivation will provide the energy needed to surmount the obstacles.

Thomas Chalmers once preached a sermon on "the expulsive power of a greater affection". A greater affection is the best motivation for change. A young man may be quite uninterested in the enhancing value of soap until he falls in love. Then disinterest seems to disappear immediately; expulsed by his new and greater affection!

Motives that encourage change

The following factors have emerged as significant:

The desire for a more satisfying and healthy way of life. (One counsellee longed to live without the limitations of constant anxiety and tension.)

The desire to achieve certain goals. (A longing to get married and have a family could give a person enough motivation to work hard at overcoming a commitment anxiety or fear of men.)

The desire to be more Christ-like in one's behaviour. (When this has motivated a person to seek counselling, however difficult and painful the path, a successful outcome is likely.)

A good motivation is one of the key factors in becoming whole. The ability to express feelings in such a way that leads to insight and healing would seem to be another.

12

IS INNER HEALING BIBLICAL?

Occasionally someone will challenge our practice of inner healing. At a recent conference, during the first session, my husband outlined the areas to be covered during the next three days. A man searched me out immediately afterwards and said that he agreed with everything that had been outlined except the inner healing seminar. "I don't believe it is biblical," he said. "Jesus has died for our sins and our sorrows. We don't need to go over it all again." The next day I spoke on the subject of personal growth. The same man approached me again. "Well you have almost persuaded me," he said, "but I still don't think it's biblical to have to feel the pain of past hurts in order to be healed; Jesus has already borne them on the cross." I was grateful for this challenge. So many people we speak to are already convinced that inner healing is just what they need, and are desperate for ministry. It could be easy to be swept along by the needs of people around one and not question the biblical validity for what one is doing.

Not everything we do in life is spelt out in scripture. That would be plainly ridiculous. But we should be sure that what we are doing does not counter the general principles of scripture. For example, the use of scanning the foetus in the womb of a mother-to-be is not specifically mentioned in the Bible, but it doesn't defy or disregard any scriptural injunctions, as would abortion for example.

So is inner healing anti-biblical as some would say it is? Or may we continue with the practice resting in the knowledge that God is in the business of healing, and that this includes the emotionally damaged, and that the method of inner healing used by many Christians today is not unscriptural?

Healing damaged emotions

Over and over again we find ourselves listening to tales of abuse and deprivation of every kind. Many times, as I have listened to a story of childhood pain, I have thought that it would have been easier to have been born without a limb than to have suffered such abuse. Jesus healed the lame, the blind, the sick. He told His disciples to go and do the same. As I sit alongside an emotionally damaged person I feel that I am praying for a sick person as much as if that person was suffering from the after-effects of a severe burning. The only difference is that the scarring is on the inside and therefore invisible. Jesus used the passage in Isaiah as His mandate. This is what He had been anointed to do:

> The Spirit of the Sovereign LORD is on me,
> because the LORD has anointed me
> to preach good news to the poor.
> He has sent me to bind up the broken-hearted,
> to proclaim freedom for the captives and release for the
>   prisoners,
> to proclaim the year of the LORD's favour
> and the day of vengeance of our God,
> to comfort all who mourn,
> and provide for those who grieve in Zion –
> to bestow on them a crown of beauty
> instead of ashes,
> the oil of gladness
> instead of mourning,
> and a garment of praise
> instead of a spirit of despair.

[Isa. 61:1–3.]

The followers of Jesus are to carry on His work. At times this will include binding up the broken-hearted and comforting those who mourn.

Growth

In many instances our work is one of encouraging growth and maturity. It is clearly God's intention that we should grow as Christians. Paul writes of this goal, "until we all . . . become mature . . . no longer infants . . . speaking the truth in love, we will in all things grow up into him" (Eph. 4:13–15).

Peter tells us, "like newborn babies, crave pure spiritual milk, so that by it you may grow up in your salvation" (1 Pet. 2:2).

James tells his readers to be glad when their faith is tested because it produces perseverance. "Perseverance must finish its work so that you may be mature and complete, not lacking anything" (Jas. 1:4).

We learn from the parable of the sower that there are many different obstacles that can prevent or block our growth. One of the reasons given for this is the thorns that grow up and choke the plant. "The seed that fell among thorns stands for those who hear, but as they go on their way they are choked by life's worries, riches and pleasures, and they do not mature" (Luke 8:14).

Much of our ministry is helping to remove the blockages to growth in people's lives. It is to do with helping to weed and clear the soil of the thorns of life that have hampered and stifled growth for one reason or another.

Catharsis

We come to my friend's statement to me that I mentioned earlier. "It isn't biblical to have to feel the pain of past hurts in order to be healed. Jesus has already borne them on the cross." My friend was able to accept prayer for inner healing, or straight biblical counselling, but not the catharsis I described as being a route to healing for some people.

The Bible gives us many examples of people being free to express their feelings of sadness and mourning: "Then Jacob tore his clothes, put on sackcloth and mourned for his son many days" (Gen. 37:34). "But King David mourned for his son every day" (2 Sam. 13:37). "I am worn out with groaning; all night long I flood my bed with weeping and drench my couch with tears" (Ps. 6:6).

As Jesus approached Jerusalem and saw the city He wept over it and said "If you, even you, had only known on this day what would bring you peace – but now it is hidden from your eyes" (Luke 19:42).

The book of Ecclesiastes tells us that, "There is a time for everything and a season for every activity under heaven . . . a time to weep and a time to laugh, a time to mourn and a time to dance" (Eccles. 3:1–4).

Biblically it is not only acceptable, but actually right, to have good feelings and bad feelings at their proper time. Didn't Jesus teach: "Blessed are those that mourn, for they will be comforted" (Matt. 5:4).

However, as we have already seen, this natural process of mourning for loss or hurt has been frequently denied, interrupted or aborted. The proper time passes and the mourning or the bad feeling is never properly experienced. Jesus said that those who mourn, who actually experience sadness and loss, would be comforted. Not those who have good cause to mourn, but don't actually experience it. To feel our feelings is part of the process of healing.

It is significant that Jesus ends the story of the unmerciful servant telling His listeners that, "This is how my heavenly Father will treat each of you unless you forgive your brother from your *heart*" (Matt. 18:35) [italics mine]. Not your mind but your heart. To forgive from the heart implies something emotional. It means actually to feel the hurt that we are forgiving. As we experience the full extent of the rejection, the loss, or the abuse we can then forgive from a standpoint of reality.

We should always be grateful to those who are ready to warn us against errors creeping into our ministry. We remember that we are dealing with an enemy who often manifests himself as an angel of light, so we should certainly exercise discernment and weigh up what we are doing in the light of Scripture.

The charge of superficiality

Another criticism sometimes levelled at the inner healing ministry is one of superficiality. The effect is said to be only temporary and relapses often occur. In some instances this is unfortunately true. How can we avoid this danger in our ministry?

1. By seeing inner healing as the responsibility of the local church where it can take its proper place as part of the church's on-going ministry to its members. So often it is seen as a one-off ministry and a quick solution to life's problems, instead of as a ministry which enables people to deal appropriately and responsibly with the obstacles to growth in their lives.

2. By putting inner healing within the context of a counselling ministry which is concerned to effect change, and to persevere until this is firmly established in a person's life.

A problem we encounter frequently is that of incest. A woman may come asking for help with a crippling fear of men and hoping for immediate relief. She may be able to express the pain of the memory, release forgiveness to the offender and experience God's love and peace, all in one session. But the protective behaviour pattern of fear may not shift immediately. Is this any wonder when you realise that this person may have lived in fear of father, brother, or uncle for perhaps five or six years? Perhaps she used to wait trembling, night after night, for those footsteps to halt outside her bedroom door. Or she may have lived for years in dread of the nights when Mummy went out to play bridge. It takes time for the nervous system to stop reacting to a stimulus created over a long period and to start responding to a new message. Often it takes months before trust is re-established and such a person is free to relate normally to men. Only hard work and persistence on the part of both counsellee and counsellor will effect the desired change of behaviour.

'The Seduction of Christianity'

In the book of this title, David Hunt and T A McMahon appear rather scathing in their criticism of psychology and inner healing. Though some of what they say may be true their personal attack on men and women of God involved in Church leadership and the healing ministry is saddening and certainly unacceptable to many readers.

"In its final evaluation *The Seduction of Christianity* is at best a misleading disservice to Christianity and at worst, a slander of the servants of God and the work of the Holy Spirit" (Peter Davids, Adjunct Professor of New Testament Theology, Regent College).

Unfortunately this book encourages division and engenders fear in the weaker and younger brethren. However it contains some timely warnings and elements of truth, especially with regard to psychology and inner healing, which are relevant to this chapter.

Psychology

Some systems of psychology may rightly be criticised as being anti-Christian in their doctrine of man and it is true that many Christians have been seduced by psychology. They have embraced its theories and practices forgetting the liberating power of the gospel. However, while psychology may be a mixed blessing, it gives many helpful insights into human personality. Some approaches are not incompatible with biblical theology and are readily adaptable in the practice of Christian pastoral caring and healing.

Roger Hurding's book *Roots and Shoots* comes as welcome reading for those who are disconcerted regarding the proper use of psychotherapy. Hurding, who lectures at an Anglican theological college with an evangelical tradition, writes with integrity and diligent research to redress the balance:

> Some Christians despair of any good coming from the counselling movement and urge us to return to the Bible, the Church Fathers or Christian tradition for all our perspectives on caring for others. I sympathise with these views but would rather argue that, for those with eyes to see, there is much within secular therapy that is an extension of God's common grace and harmonises with his revealed word. There is a great need for those of us with Christian convictions to sift the methodologies on offer so that we may discern evidences of the Kingdom. In doing this we aim at an integration of valid psychological and theological insight. Such an enterprise would not be a mere academic exercise but an attempt to bring the love of the Father, the fellowship of the Son and the healing power of the Spirit into every part of the lives we seek to help.

Visualisation

"To make visible, to picture, call up a clear mental image" (*Chambers Everyday Dictionary*).

The technique of visualisation as practised by psychic healers, sorcerers and witch-doctors is rightly criticised by Hunt and McMahon. In this case visualisation is an attempt to create or manipulate the physical world. It is the use of the mental powers to create one's own reality. Occasionally one hears of inner healing techniques which border on this. Where healing of the memories changes an actual memory by picturing or visualising something that never happened, it is not healing; it is an escape from reality and an avoidance of truth. However, God is the creator of our minds and has given us the powers of imagination and visualisation. To denigrate these powers as "mental alchemy" could be to miss a God-given channel of healing. Jesus is the Truth (John 14:6) and the Holy Spirit leads us into all truth (John 16:13). Frequently, during the ministry of inner healing a past trauma is uncovered and with the memory comes the realisation that Jesus, who said "I am with you always" (Matt. 28:20, Living Bible), was there; if the Holy Spirit takes the blinkers off and allows us to see the truth of His healing presence at the scene of the trauma, this is God-given healing and we should give Him the glory.

People's minds can be vehicles for good or evil. God speaks to us and so does Satan. We have a good example of this in the life of Peter. Jesus asked Peter who he thought He was and Peter answered Him, "You are the Christ, the Son of the living God." Jesus replied, "Blessed are you, Simon son of Jonah, for this was not revealed to you by man, but by my Father in heaven." In the same chapter in Matthew we find Peter rebuking Jesus for predicting His death. "Never, Lord!" he said. "This shall never happen to you!" Jesus turned and said to Peter, "Out of my sight Satan! You are a stumbling block to me; you do not have in mind the things of God, but the things of men" (Matt. 16:13–23).

Our minds, like Peter's, can be used for both good and evil. Visualisation techniques have been used in psychic healings and by sorcerers of all kinds but this is not a reason for throwing the baby out with the bath water. Repeatedly we have seen how God can use a person's imagination supernaturally and give him a picture that has contained both the truth of Scripture and the truth about himself.

Where our memories of the past are visual they will come into our minds in picture form. As God brings these memories to the surface He often applies His healing with visual symbolism too. I remember praying with a very depressed woman and asking God to reach down into the pit where she was. It was moving to watch her downcast face gradually turn upwards; her clenched hand unfold and reach up to take the hand of God as, in her mind, she saw Him reach down to her and draw her up. I was about to read some appropriate Scriptures to her but instead, God spoke sovereignly to her using a visual picture for her healing.

Inner healing

This is severely undermined in *The Seduction of Christianity*.

> Inner healing is simply a Christianised psychoanalysis that uses the power of suggestion to 'solve problems' which it has oftentimes actually created . . .
> Such has been the case with many sincere Christians who have become the victims of inner healing. The glowing testimonies hide this very real problem. In churches where inner healing has begun to be practised, members who seemed quite normal and happy in their Christian life have become depressed after accepting the destructive idea that they were in fact driven by deeply buried hurts and resentments of which they were not even aware. The healing-of-memories process that was intended to deliver them has in fact created many pseudomemories that have confused them.

It may of course be true that suggestive and manipulative practices have developed in some ministries. It may also be true that some people have not been helped by inner healing prayer and in fact may seem worse after such ministry. But it is doubtful that the ministry of inner healing caused the resulting depression or neurosis. It may have brought it to light but would not be the cause. Also to suggest that a person is the victim of inner healing is to take away self responsibility. A person is only a victim if something is done to him against his will. No one *has* to receive prayer for inner healing. However we should have wisdom as to whom we agree to pray for. As I pointed out in *Set My People Free* (p.107), "Some people are definitely unsuitable candidates for this particular ministry. That is not to say they do not need help, but for them it may come simply in the form of loving relationships, straightforward biblical counselling sessions, or maybe referral to a professional."

Peter Davids responds helpfully to the unjust attacks on inner healing. "In criticising inner healing as sorcery and opening the mind to demonic guides, does Hunt have any awareness that this does in fact happen? We know what happens when people play with the occult: they get demonised. Anyone who expels demons knows full well that many of them got in because a person (or his family) opened himself to the occult. The clinical evidence is consistent with the theory. What evidence does Hunt present that this is just as true of inner healing? In fact, the clinical evidence is not consistent with Hunt's theory. After inner healing people regularly want to pray more, love God more, love others more, read their Bible more, etc. Is this the fruit of the devil? Is the devil now producing God's works? On the one hand, Hunt is right to criticise mere pragmatism, a 'But it works!' approach, but Jesus said, 'By their fruits you shall know them.' Surely there are folk who minister inner healing who are kooks and cranks, just as there are preachers who are wrong headed. But, by and large, what is the fruit of inner healing? From our pastoral practice we assert that it is the fruit of the Spirit or also a good imitation of it" (Review by Dr Peter H Davids, *Charisma* 1986).

We are free in Christ. He comes into our lives and hearts the day we are born again. Unfortunately many damaged and hurting individuals cannot appropriate the freedom that is theirs. They seem unable to possess their possessions. They read and understand the truth but their experience is nowhere near what they read. They live in prisons of depression, anxiety and fear, while longing for freedom. Inner healing is an attempt to help such a person appropriate this freedom in his heart as well as in his mind.

13

DEMONISATION AND INNER HEALING

It would be easier to leave on one side the thorny question of the relationship between the deliverance ministry and emotional healing. However it is a subject that has to be tackled sooner or later by any church involved in a ministry of healing. We live in a world where emotional damage and mental illness are on the increase. Nevertheless the Bible clearly points to demonic activity as being part of the predicament for some fallen human beings. In many places we find Jesus healing the sick and casting out demons. He sends out the twelve to do likewise and then the seventy-two did it also. Casting out demons is part of the work of a disciple. However we are all limited by our world view and our finite minds. We only see, at present, "through a glass darkly," and our knowledge is incomplete. To complicate matters, being uniquely individual we each see things from distinct perspectives. It is as if we were looking into a room through opposite windows. We would all be seeing the same room but from various angles. Our description of what we see may lead us to believe we were viewing a different room from the other people. The problem is that our vantage point is distinct, personal and limited.

The subject is difficult because our insights are limited and our perspectives are different. None of us has the whole truth; none of us is infallible. But whilst differing viewpoints abound, the danger is for us to wear blinkers and hold firmly to our own point of view regardless of what others may be perceiving.

One view would be that all psychological problems are basically demonic and deliverance ministry would therefore be appropriate in every case. Problems such as gluttony, pornography, homosexuality, adultery, kleptomania, as well as feelings such as rejection, fear, jealousy, bitterness, anger, would be seen to be caused by evil spirits.

A second view is that most of our problems are derived from wrong thinking or emotional damage. Therefore counselling or inner healing would seem the answer.

Yet another view is that a person's problems could be caused by both simultaneously. Differences would then arise amongst counsellors as to which you should tackle first – deliverance or inner healing.

Our perspective to date, though still open to change, is that everyone has some emotional damage by the mere fact of being born into a fallen world and having imperfect parents. Our basic needs may have been inadequately met resulting in emotional trauma. Therefore emotional problems can never be ruled out and are usually present to a greater or lesser degree in all of us.

Nevertheless, Satan is still active in the world today and we have all been, and will continue to be, victimised by him. Jesus called him "the ruler of this world"; the world that we are at present living in. Therefore we cannot rule out his activity in a person's life, though the degree of influence he exerts varies from person to person.

Satan is able to take advantage of all the negative situations of life. Emotional hurt may open us up to oppression from the enemy. Habitual sin may give him a foothold. Spiritual rebellion by involvement with the occult gives him access. Long held attitudes of bitterness, resentment and unforgiveness can leave loopholes for him.

Within this framework we find our problems are twofold. One is discerning the presence of a spirit and the other is the order of priority between healing and deliverance.

For example a young man described his homosexual tendencies which were accompanied by a fear of women. On questioning him a dominating mother seemed to be at the root of his problems. But I needed discernment to know whether he was also being kept in bondage to the inclination and the fear by an unclean spirit. Would the problem be solved by inner healing and some counselling or would we also need to exercise a deliverance ministry?

On one occasion, during a service, a woman fell to the ground under the power of the Holy Spirit and began shaking and jerking quite violently. Her breathing was rapid and she appeared to be in pain. Those ministering needed discernment to decide on the appropriate way to minister to her at that moment. God was at work, but His power seemed to be encountering a resistance, or blockage which was causing this particular manifestation. The task was to find out whether this was demonic or the surfacing of an emotional trauma.

The priority of healing over deliverance may be a cause of contention between those ministering. The question is which should come first? Is there any point in trying to heal a person of a fear of death when a spirit of fear is also oppressing him? Or vice versa. Is there any point in commanding a spirit to go in Jesus' name whilst a foothold of hurt remains giving the demon a protected nook and a reason to stay?

These are real problems that often confront those who seek to minister healing to the sick; to discern whether the sickness be emotional, physical or spiritual. We suggest some guidelines that may help us through the maze of opinions.

Guidelines

1. Remember the limitations of lay ministry in a local church

a) Though you may be called to pray for people from other churches at open meetings, it is not wise to minister further to people from other churches or people whose pastoral care is the responsibility of others, unless so requested by those holding such responsibility and who will provide the on-going care which may be necessary.

b) It is not wise to minister to those who are being treated professionally or are beyond our expertise and should be referred to a professional. Assistance could be requested by the professional in charge; this might take the form of support, prayer, or occasionally a deliverance ministry, which the doctor feels he is not equipped to undertake. Usually this takes place under the direction or authority of the leadership of the church.

c) Special care needs to be taken if a person has a history of mental illness. Sometimes we have to realise that though we suspect demonic oppression this may not be the most serious problem the person has, nor the problem which takes priority. The leadership of the church should always be involved with any ministry to such a person.

2. Remember the manifestation may not be demonic

At a recent conference a young girl asked for prayer. Her problem was a long-standing one of fear and anxiety. She was involved in helping others and had good insight into her own problems, though no ministry to date had penetrated to their roots.

The power of God was present that evening and in a short time she was manifesting a great deal of pain. She said it came from deep within and was causing her whole body to contort. On seeing this manifestation one of those ministering began to suggest that she should be delivered of various spirits.

Talking to me afterwards the young girl expressed mixed feelings of anger, despair and shame. She was angry that no one had understood enough of what was happening to help her express the deep pain and anguish that the Holy Spirit was surfacing. She felt despair that an opportunity had been missed to bring her nearer to solving her problem and she felt shame because the ministry had seemed to strip her naked and rob her of dignity.

Manifestation of emotional pain can be quite violent. It

may cause the person to gag, choke or clench his teeth. It may shake the body or cause it to go rigid. These may be accompanied by loud cries or low moaning.

Demonic oppression on the other hand usually manifests in a rather different way. The focus of pain seems to move about the body, the noise is more unnatural, the eyes often turn upwards (though this is not proof), the voice changes and speaks in a threatening or mocking or blaspheming way. Frequently there is a bad odour. The face may reflect a leering visage.

3. Remember one could be wrong

A word of knowledge or discernment should always be tested before offering it to the sufferer. Nor should it be insisted upon if it is not received by the others ministering or the person being ministered to. For example to suggest to a person that he is controlled, oppressed or possessed by a spirit of witchcraft or incest from an unknown ancestor, would seem inappropriate – even damaging. It can never be proved one way or the other and may leave the person feeling worried, condemned or contaminated. In any case it is not necessary always to know the name or cause of an oppression. Often I have heard my husband, David, speak to the "darkness within" telling it to go in the Name of Jesus. He has spoken quietly but firmly and usually there has been an immediate release.

4. Remember that one can ask questions

Those ministering may ask questions of each other but also it is always good to ask the person being ministered to what is happening. Find out how he feels and if God is showing him anything. Never suggest that anyone's problem is demonic without:

- a clear manifestation
- confirmation from other people
- an acknowledgement and willingness to proceed from the person receiving ministry

5. Remember co-operation from the person concerned is vital

Without this co-operation much time and energy will be wasted. If a demon does not leave immediately it is told to go in the Name of Jesus then stop the ministry and find out why. Either it has some foothold or the diagnosis is incorrect.

6. Remember that deliverance is not the end of the ministry

Deliverance is just one part of ministry to a person. It is not the whole story. Arrange to spend further time with that person for healing the damage or dealing with the sin that gave the demon a foothold. Discuss new behaviour patterns or any wrong thinking that needs changing. Bear in mind the story Jesus told about the spirit leaving a man and returning to find the house swept and clean but obviously vacant. He finds seven other spirits and they go and live there (Luke 11:24–26). If a spirit of lust has dominated a man's thinking and behaving, not only is repentance, cleansing and filling of the Holy Spirit important but he needs to renew the mind with new thinking, and his time with new behaviour or "the final condition of that man is worse than the first".

7. Remember which values are fundamental to this ministry

"Values are like the foundations of a building. The deeper and firmer the foundations the better one can build. Without good foundations a house stands in danger of collapse" (*Set My People Free*, p. 28).

Our values in this ministry are:

– the work of the Holy Spirit
– the authority of the name of Jesus
– the word of God
– love
– growth of the individual (both spiritual and emotional)
– the body of Christ

The value to be most desired here is the one of love. So many people have been badly hurt during their lifetime. We must not add to their hurt by insensitive and thoughtless ministry. When Jesus was asked which was the greatest command He replied, " 'Love the Lord your God . . .' and the second is like it: 'Love . . . your neighbour as yourself.' All the Law and the Prophets hang on these two commandments" (Matt. 22:37–40).

"Love your neighbour as yourself." Bearing in mind this command we must ask ourselves the following questions:

Is this the right sort of ministry for this person?
Would I like this to be done to me?
Is this the best time for this ministry?
Is this the best place for this ministry?
Am I protecting this person's dignity and treating him as one of God's children?
What is the most loving way of handling this problem?

After the outpouring of the Holy Spirit that we experienced at St. Andrew's in 1981, some of us immediately presumed that any strange manifestation was demonic. At that time we began casting out spirits of fear, anger, lust etc., but many of those we ministered to did not show any marked improvement. Time was the test. On the other hand beneficial results have been seen in those who have continued with a longer, more gentle ministry that has mostly addressed the hurts of the past. This ministry involves the counsellee in taking responsibility for sin, for renouncing wrong choices or inner vows and for deciding to walk in new ways. Then, provided the counsellor believes it right (it would not be automatic by any means), he would deal with any bondage or oppression, having first assured himself that any footholds that could harbour a spirit were gone.

This would seem the most loving way of ministering to one of God's children.

14

ARRIVAL AT A SAFER PLACE

Counselling is a vehicle that should be moving towards a destination. The vehicle is necessary for the journey but once the destination is reached it can be abandoned. It is important, therefore, that a counsellor be alert to indications that the end is in sight. Once a counsellee has reached a place of greater safety within himself, within the body of Christ and with God, the need for counselling is over – the destination has been reached. This is not to say that a counsellee cannot ever return for help should difficulties arise at a future date.

Security within

It is amazing how many people enter counselling and admit to either feeling as though they were two personalities or of having an unknown part of themselves hidden away. It is a part they are afraid of. It is full of bad feelings. It should be kept out of sight. Frequently the picture that comes into their minds as we pray is of a child locked in a cave or cupboard; an unacceptable child; a bad child, who is impossible to love. On the same day recently, I prayed with two women. One saw the child in a dark cave behind thick wooden doors and the other saw her in a closet. Both felt the need to keep the child firmly locked away because she was so revolting and stupid. Both women were ashamed of the child they saw.

It seems that some of the feelings of childhood are too

difficult to handle and so the child splits away from them, leaving them in some crypt in the lower precincts of his personality. The child continues to grow into adulthood unaware that he has left behind a part of himself, truncated at whatever age the split occurred, still with the unresolved feelings. Integration of this "unacceptable child" with the "adult" is one of the goals of counselling.

The following extract is from the diary of a counsellee nearing the termination of counselling.

> In retrospect I find it difficult to remember the early days of ministry, except I slept for hours afterwards. It was probably due to those two main emotions being flushed out, dealt with and exposed to the light. Each remembrance was a birthing – I hate thinking of the relationship between the physical birth and inner healing but that's where it's at – a prolonged painful process and when the emotion is out finally – that's it. Then there is a period of stabilisation. I know I must be in the toddler stage – reeling from chair to coffee table – a bit uncertainly but toddling beats crawling on one's hands and knees!

In the initial stages this counsellee was quite out of touch with her "inner child". Gradually the "child" with all her hurts became apparent and she went through a period of non-acceptance and self-loathing. When this note was written an integration was taking place and the "child" was becoming an accepted part of the "adult".

A recent TV film, *Nobody's Child* told the harrowing but true story of Marie Balter, a young woman diagnosed as schizophrenic and institutionalised for twenty years. She was in fact suffering from acute anxiety caused by a very abused childhood. The helpless, fearful child she once was is easily conjured up and continually takes control of the adult, rendering her incapable of living normally. She recovers slowly and painfully, constantly battling with anxiety and attacks of panic; the terrified child ever ready to overwhelm her.

Marie's healing is aided by the support of good friends and her loving husband. It is finally achieved, however, when her husband, Joe, suddenly dies leaving her alone. The old anxiety threatens to come back and she once again has a picture of the little girl standing in front of her looking lost and bedraggled. In the past the sight of this child had always caused Marie to panic and lose control, but on this occasion she looks at the child, smiles at her and as she does so the child changes and is seen kneeling on the bed, clean and pretty. The "adult Marie" approaches the "child Marie" and begins to stroke her. She then takes the child in her arms and they lie down on the bed together.

The "adult" embraces the "child"; takes responsibility for her and starts to care for her. The "child" integrates with the "adult" – they become one.

This integration in the life of a counsellee is marked by an acceptance of the childish, feeling part of himself. The "adult" has learned how to live and cope with the needy, the fearful, the angry and the anxious feelings. No longer will there be the need for suppression or inappropriate expression. Now there can be appropriate control and openness.

A good illustration of how to deal with difficult feelings was recently provided for me by a counselling colleague. She called me one morning to say that she had just received some very bad news and that she might be a little late for a number of counselling appointments we had together. She eventually arrived and we settled down to work. She appeared to be totally involved with the job in hand. The next day, however, she asked me if I could spare her some time. We spent an hour together and she was able to work through the difficult feelings that had been aroused by the previous day's bad news concerning the tragic massacre of some of her friends in a Christian community in Zimbabwe. The anger and pain of loss were not suppressed or denied but controlled until there was an appropriate opportunity to express them and receive some healing.

Once a counsellee has come to this place of inner security and at-oneness within himself the need for on-going counselling is approaching an end.

Security in the body of Christ

A counsellee should leave counselling not only more at one with himself, but he should feel himself a more integrated member of the body of Christ.

Distancing and isolation from others is frequently a side-effect of inner disharmony. People in pain have a problem making close adult relationships. They become either loners or are childishly and exclusively dependent on one or two others.

One such person always sat at the back of the church on his own. He never stayed to coffee after the services and appeared to have no friends. Some time went by and I became aware of some significant changes in his behaviour. Then, quite spontaneously, he told me how much help he was receiving through being counselled by a couple in the church. He looked more relaxed, began to stay around longer and make some friends. Some time later as if to cap it all, I heard that he had become a leader of a group.

Once this integration with the family of God has begun a counsellee will soon be able to manage without the support of the counselling relationship.

Lastly, the really happy ending to counselling comes when a counsellee has found not only a greater degree of safety within himself and safety in the body of Christ, but most of all safety with God.

Security in the knowledge and love of God

"I don't feel as if I belong anywhere."
"I'm not special to anyone."
"I feel so lonely."
"People always let me down."
"I feel so anxious all the time."

These comments and many more like them are spoken daily in our "upper-room". They are honest admissions of painful needs which exist within the human heart; needs to belong, to be loved, to be special, to be safe. Such normal, human needs, but they seem impossible to meet in the absolute way that would reassure and satisfy.

It is hard for any human being, hurting or not, to accept the limited and relative nature of human love. We want our mother, our father, our spouse, our friend, to be perfect. We want their total understanding, their perpetual patience, their unconditional love and their constant loyalty. We cannot accept their weaknesses and failures and blame them for letting us down by their human frailty. It's hard to forgive someone who was not there when we needed him, who didn't pick up our unspoken message for help, who failed to ransom our wobbly self-worth.

"What is the meaning of this nostalgia for perfection which some admit and others hide, but which is inevitably there in every man and woman? It is our home-sickness for Paradise. The place we are all looking for is the Paradise we have lost. The whole of humanity suffers from what we might call the 'Paradise Lost' complex" (*A Place for You*, Paul Tournier).

A child who has experienced "good enough" mothering will be more equipped to meet the disappointments, frustrations and separations of this "paradise lost" situation. Without the experience of good parenting a child is left with his cup of security and self-worth only half full. He may then spend his life desperately hoping to get it filled or he may decide that the struggle is hopeless and sink into a grey depression.

Though real Christian community and true friendship are necessary ingredients towards healing the disappointments and deprivations of a person's early life, they will never completely satisfy the heart of man.

Christian pastoral counselling and inner healing will ultimately fail unless those who seek help are lovingly pointed in the direction of the safest place of all – the Heart of God. Yes, we all need to face our past; the way we perceived it and our reactions to it. We also need to forgive the painful inadequacies of those around us; those who have failed, both past and present, to appease our hunger to belong and to be loved. Ministry cannot end there. We must help those who come for help to discover and participate in the riches of God's love.

Many seek anxiously for a place of safety. They lie awake at night fearful of the coming day. King David had many such nights but he discovered a safe place and was able to say, "You [God] are my hiding place" (Ps. 32:7), and "He is my shield and the horn of my salvation, my stronghold" (Ps. 18:2). When this becomes a reality, anxiety and fear are driven back.

There are others who long for a dependable relationship with someone who means what he says. But even the closest relationship can fail. David, who knew all about that too, was able to say, "Though my father and mother forsake me the LORD will receive me" (Ps. 27:10). It is not in God's character to fail or forsake us.

Others have never had the experience of being special to anyone and have consequently felt there must be something wrong with them. Only the truth of their "specialness" to God their Heavenly Father will overcome that nagging fear. The Bible teaches that we are each of us special to Him. "Can a mother forget the baby at her breast and have no compassion on the child she has borne? Though she may forget, I will not forget you! See, I have engraved you on the palms of my hands" (Isa. 49:15,16).

In several places God calls His people, "the apple of his eye". Zechariah says, "Whoever touches you touches the apple of his eye" (Zech. 2:8). This expression gives the sense of a doting parent hovering over a very special child.

When a counsellee believes this to be God's attitude to him his half empty cup will soon fill up and overflow the brim. As Jesus longed over Jerusalem so I believe He longs over many of His children today, desiring to gather them together, "as a hen gathers her chicks under her wings" (Luke 13:34).

Though he may need a safe place in which to discover these truths, ultimately the only truly safe place is "under the shadow of his wings". Once this has become a reality it is time to bring a closure to the counselling relationship – it has served its purpose and the goal has been achieved.

BIBLIOGRAPHY

This list follows the order in which these titles are
first mentioned

The Presenting Past, Michael Jacobs. Harper & Row Publ.,
1985

The Haven of the Masses, Christian Lalive d'Epinay.
Billing & Sons Ltd, 1969

The Different Drum, Scott Peck. Simon and Schuster, 1987

Fully Human, Fully Alive, John Powell. Argus Communi-
cations, 1976

A Case for Personal Psychotherapy, Peter Lomas. Oxford
University Press, 1981

Dibs, In Search of Self, Virginia Axline. Penguin Books,
1964

The Broken Image, Leanne Payne. Crossway Books, 1981

On Becoming a Person, Carl Rogers. Houghton Mifflin
Co., 1961

Will the Real Me Please Stand Up, John Powell. Tabor
Publishing, 1985

The Dynamics of Religion, Bruce Reed. Darton, Longman
and Todd, 1978

Emotional Expression in Psychotherapy, Pierce, Nichols
and DuBrin. Gardner Press, 1983

Families and How to Survive Them, John Cleese and Robin
Skynner. Methuen, 1983

One Child, Torey Hayden. Souvenir Press, 1981

Clinical Theology, Frank Lake. Darton, Longman and
Todd (Abridged Version), 1981

Tight Corners in Pastoral Counselling, Frank Lake. Darton, Longman and Todd, 1981

Touching, The Human Significance of the Skin, Ashley Montagu. Harper-Row Publishers, 1971

I'm OK – You're OK, T A Harris. Pan Books, 1973

Prisoners of Pain, Arthur Janov. Abacus, 1982

The Little Book of Hugs, Kathleen Keating. Angus and Robertson, 1983

Roots and Shoots, Roger Hurding. Hodder and Stoughton, 1985

Telling the Truth to Troubled Minds, William Backus. Bethany House Publ., 1985

A Tool for Christians (Books 1 & 2), Jean Morrison. Dept. of Educ. of the Church of Scotland, 1980

Gestalt Is, J O Stevens. Real People Press, 1975

Friend to Friend, David Stone & Larry Keefauver. Group Books.

The Seduction of Christianity, David Hunt and T A McMahon. Harvest House Publishers, 1985

A Place for You, Paul Tournier. SCM Press Ltd., 1968